CW00542668

The Soap Quiz Book

Compiled by
Mark Bennison

Forewords by
Tom Watt
and
Sue Jenkins

First published in 2009
This edition published in 2016 by
Apex Publishing Ltd
12A St. John's Road, Clacton on Sea
Essex, CO15 4BP, United Kingdom
www.apexpublishing.co.uk

Typography and layout by
Andrews UK Limited
www.andrewsuk.com

Please email any queries to Chris Cowlin
mail@apexpublishing.co.uk

Copyright © 2011, 2016 Mark Bennison
The author has asserted his moral rights

Cover Design: Siobhan Smith

All rights reserved. This book is sold subject to the
condition, that no part of this book is to be reproduced,
in any shape or form. Or by way of trade, stored in a
retrieval system or transmitted in any form or by any
means, electronic, mechanical, photocopying, recording,
be lent, re-sold, hired out or otherwise circulated in any
form of binding or cover other than that in which it is
published and without a similar condition, including this
condition being imposed on the subsequent purchaser,
without prior permission of the copyright holder.

Contents

Foreword

by Tom Watt

It's a long time ago now that we started life in Albert Square. I won't say how long because it might give one of the EastEnders answers away later in the quiz book! All I will say is that, as an actor, the three years I spent on the BBC soap were some of the most enjoyable of my career: great writing, a really good cast and a fantastic character to play, 'Lofty'.

None of us knew then how successful EastEnders would be. But we got our answer pretty quickly. It seemed like no time at all before we were getting 20 million people at a time tuning in to find out what happened next. I even remember reading in one newspaper the comment that 'the only unrealistic thing about Brookside (the groundbreaking Channel 4 soap) is that none of the characters are talking about what's happening in EastEnders!'

Coronation Street, of course, has a long and distinguished history and is still going strong. Since the mid-80s, though, it's had plenty of competition for the public's affections. It sometimes seems as if everybody watches one soap or another, sometimes more than one. And they can keep up with what's happening in the ones they don't watch by talking to their friends who do.

There have been plenty of famous storylines and famous characters. And that's why I hope 'The Soap Quiz Book' will be fun: a chance to test yourself, your family and friends and to find out just how well you remember what's happened in Albert Square or the Rovers Return, in Emmerdale or Ramsey Street, over the years.

I expect there are some questions in here that I really ought to know the answers to but don't! I'm sure there are a few 'masterminds' out there who'll fancy their chances of getting every single one right. Either way, hope you'll enjoy the quizzes as much as you've enjoyed watching the soaps that all the questions are based round.

Oh, and before I go, one last thing: thanks to Apex Publishing Ltd, the publishers of this book, for agreeing to pay a royalty on sales of the book to Children In Need.

Best wishes
Tom Watt

Foreword

by Sue Jenkins

I have been an actress for over thirty years, working in theatres in London and in the provinces as well as playing many roles on television. It is however, the characters I played in Soap Operas that people seem to remember more than anything else. I played 'Gloria Todd' in 'Coronation Street' for four years, I then moved onto 'Brookside' where I played the long suffering 'Jackie Corkhill' for eleven years and have recently appeared in 'Emmerdale' and 'Doctors'.

Soap operas are some of the nations' favourite form of entertainment, attracting huge television audiences. Coronation Street, Emmerdale, Eastenders, Hollyoaks and the daytime favourite Doctors, to name but a few, we seem to have room for them all. However, as any soap fan will know, sometimes the storylines are more interesting than others and sometimes they seem rather far-fetched with outrageous plots and extraordinary characters.

Soaps enter our houses like old familiar friends, no need for an introduction, they are expected and their daily arrival (gone are the days of just one or two episodes a week) is much anticipated. We laugh and cry with the characters, loathing some and loving others, yes, just like old friends!

The plots are the source of even further entertainment, long after the episodes have finished, as we discuss and debate the rights and wrongs, the will he, won't he? should she, shouldn't she?

Then there are the soap quizzes! I remember being on a TV quiz years ago and being questioned on 'Brookside' (assuming I would be a fountain of knowledge). How wrong they were... I might have been in the show for eleven years but could hardly remember any actual events and names of characters were a distant memory!

I hope your memories of soap happenings are better than mine. I do remember one very important thing about the world of Soap, I met and worked with some wonderful and highly talented people and had the opportunity to play the gammet of emotions in some heartbreaking scenes. I enjoyed working as part of a team and the great sense of 'belonging'. For all this, and the regular income, I shall always be extremely grateful.

Good luck with this quiz book …

Best wishes
Sue Jenkins

The Soap Quiz Book

Questions

Eastenders

1. In what year was the first ever episode screened – 1993, 1985 or 1987?

2. Can you name the producer/script-editor team that created EastEnders?

3. Which iconic building has the address of 46 Albert Square?

4. Can you name the wartime spin-off first aired in 1988?

5. Can you recall the names of two roads outside Albert Square?

6. Who was the original landlord of the Queen Victoria public house? Ange ,

7. What is the name of the bench in Albert Square's garden?

8. On which day did Pauline Fowler die in 2006?

9. Which Spice Girl appeared in the soap in 1992?

10. Who shot Phil Mitchell? Cindy

Coronation Street

11. In what year was Coronation Street first broadcast? 1963

12. Who created the show?

13. Which television production company broadcasts Coronation Street?

14. In which fictional town in Greater Manchester is Coronation Street set?

15. Coronation Street was the final choice of name for the show, but what other name was considered – Jubilee Street, Silver Street or Queen Street?

16. Coronation Street incorporates the residents of three neighbouring streets. Can you name one of them?

17. True or false: Elsie Tanner was known as 'the tart with the heart' in the 1960s?

18. What is the name of the newsagents on Coronation Street?

19. Which long-serving character of 34 years died in 2008 before moving to Blackpool?

20. Who composed the theme music for Coronation Street – Eric Spearman, Eric Spear or Eric Spearson?

Emmerdale

21. In what year was the first episode of Emmerdale broadcast
    – 1987, 1988 or 1989?

22. What was the title of the show before it was changed to
    Emmerdale? Farm

23. What was the name of the original village?

24. Which family lived at and ran Emmerdale Farm?
    Sugdens

25. Which family spearheaded the revamped Emmerdale and
    owned Home Farm? Tates.

26. Which storyline disaster in 1993 brought Emmerdale into
    the public eye, producing its highest-ever viewing figure of
    18.6 million? Aeroplan Crash.

27. Which anniversary did Emmerdale celebrate in 2007,
    marked by a huge explosion ripping through Annie's cottage
    caused by Victoria Sugden – 25, 30 or 35 years?

28. Which two flamboyant and materialistic characters were
    married in the 5000th episode?

29. Who is the longest-serving current character – Eric Pollard,
    Alan Turner or Betty Eagleton?

30. Who killed Tom King?

Hollyoaks

31. In which country is Hollyoaks a television soap opera – Australia, United Kingdom or America?

32. In which year was Hollyoaks first broadcast – 1995, 1997 or 1999?

33. Hollyoaks is a fictional suburb of Chester, in which county – Cheshire, Warwickshire or Hampshire?

34. What is the name of the only character that has remained in the show since Hollyoaks first started?

35. How many spin-offs of Hollyoaks have been created – 2, 3 or 4?

36. True or false: Hollyoaks produces fragrances for men and women?

37. Who was responsible for Max Cunningham's death?

38. Following on from the previous question, in which Hollyoaks spin-off did Niall Rafferty fall to his death?

39. In 2008, how many awards did Hollyoaks win at the British Soap Awards?

40. What is the name of the local higher education college?

Neighbours

41. In what year was the first ever episode of Neighbours screened – 1985, 1987 or 1989?

42. Which Australian television producer created Neighbours as well as The Young Doctors and Sons and Daughters?

43. Which British composer, who was involved in Crossroads and moved to Australia in 1992, composed the theme music for Neighbours?

44. In which fictitious middle-class Australian suburb is Ramsay Street situated?

45. How many houses are there in the Ramsay Street cul-de-sac – 4, 6 or 8?

46. The show originally focused on which two families?

47. In what year in the 1980s did Neighbours come to BBC1?

48. Which now mega-famous female singer played the character of Charlene Robinson?

49. Which character has appeared in the soap ever since the first episode – Harold Bishop, Paul Robinson or Lou Carpenter?

50. In 1991, which character was swept out to sea?

Home And Away

51. Home and Away premiered in which year – 1987, 1988 or 1989?

52. In which Australian city, famous for the Opera House, is Home and Away produced?

53. The show originally focused on which two characters, who ran the Summer Bay Caravan Park and lived there with a succession of foster children?

54. As Home and Away expanded, which family became the main focus of attention?

55. Who created Home and Away – Alan Bates, Alan Bateman or Alan Batley?

56. True or false: Home and Away drew its inspiration from a stop-off in Kangaroo Point?

57. How many versions of the theme song have there been – 5, 7 or 9?

58. Which one of the Minogue sisters appeared in the show between 1989 and 1990?

59. Which 'flaming mongrels' character has been in Home and Away since the beginning?

60. In 2008, who was shot in the chest on a construction site and left for dead?

Doctors

61.   In which year was the first episode of Doctors screened –
       1998, 2000 or 2002?

62.   What is the name of the health centre?

63.   True or false: Doctors is the only soap that gives each
       episode a title?

64.   How long did Christopher Timothy stay with the show – 6,
       8 or 10 years?

65.   Can you give the first names of the current three most
       popular characters?

66.   In which country did Dr Brendan 'Mac' McGuire and Kate
       end up?

67.   Which actor, who played Mark Fowler in EastEnders,
       directed three episodes of Doctors?

68.   Which policeman, who is not considered as a regular, is the
       longest-serving character?

69.   Which character was held at a gunpoint in his role as a
       solicitor?

70.   Who killed Katya – Carter, Squires or Leo?

Casualty

71. In which year was Casualty first broadcast – 1986, 1987 or 1988?

72. True or false: Casualty is the longest-running emergency medical drama series in the world?

73. Casualty is based around which fictional hospital?

74. Following on from the previous question, on which hospital department does the programme focus?

75. Can you name the two men that created Casualty?

76. True or false: Casualty boasts that it has featured more future stars than any other UK soap or drama series?

77. What is the name of the spin-off series that focuses on the police service of Holby?

78. Can you name the charge nurse who has appeared in the show since it first began?

79. The cast of the show released the single 'Everlasting Love', which peaked at what number in the UK chart in 1998 – 1, 3 or 5?

80. Who composed the theme music for Casualty – Alan Freeman, Ken Freeman or Josh Freeman?

Holby City

81. In which year was the first episode of Holby City screened – 1997, 1999 or 2001?

82. Can you name the two creators of Holby City?

83. Holby City is set in which fictional county close to the Welsh boarder?

84. Can you name the three wards featured in Holby City?

85. Can you name the sexy ward sister who is the longest-serving character?

86. In 2008, which award did Holby City win, beating EastEnders, Emmerdale and The Bill?

87. True or false: Lola's ex-husband is Ric Griffin?

88. Can you name the two Holby City actors who were formerly in EastEnders?

89. Which consultant nurse character had a coke addiction?

90. At Christmas 2004, what crashing vehicle caused an explosion at the hospital?

The Bill

91. In which year was The Bill first broadcast – 1992, 1993 or 1994?

92. True or false: The Bill gets its name from a slang term for the police?

93. Who created The Bill – Steve McQueen, Geoff McQueen or Freddie McQueen?

94. The Bill is set around which police station?

95. Following on from the previous question, in which fictional London Borough is the police station located?

96. Which actor, who played DC Alfred 'Tosh' Lines, died as a result of alcohol abuse in 1998?

97. True or false: Vic Gallucci, who played DC Tom Baker, is in the Guinness Book of Records for the most walk-on parts?

98. Which Spice Girl appeared in The Bill in 1993 as a troubled teenager named Janice?

99. The actress who plays PC Beth Green starred in which other soap prior to joining The Bill?

100. How many spin-off programmes have been created from The Bill – 2, 3 or 4?

Leslie Grantham

101. In which year was Leslie Grantham born – 1945, 1947 or 1949?

102. True or false: Leslie is a born East Ender?

103. In which regiment of the British Army did Leslie enlist?

104. True or false: Leslie was convicted of murder?

105. In which BBC science fiction series did Leslie make his first TV appearance as Kiston in 1984?

106. In total, for how many years was Leslie associated with 'Dirty Den' – 10, 15 or 20?

107. After EastEnders, which TV police drama did Leslie appear in as Jimmy Collins?

108. What was the name of Leslie's character in The Paradise Club?

109. What is the title of Leslie's autobiography?

110. True or false: Leslie supports West Ham United football club?

Mike Reid

111. Mike Reid is best known for his role in which soap opera?

112. Following on from the previous question, what was the name of Mike Reid's character?

113. In which year was Mike Reid born – 1940, 1941 or 1942?

114. True or false: Mike Reid's first job in entertainment was as a stand-up comedian?

115. What was the title of the one-off hit record that Mike Reid recorded in 1975, which reached number 10 in the singles chart?

116. Following on from question 111, in which year did Mike Reid join the cast of this soap – 1985, 1987 or 1989?

117. Following on from the previous question, in which year did Mike Reid leave the programme – 1996, 1998 or 2000?

118. True or false: Mike Reid was a born East Ender?

119. Which sport was Mike Reid's passion – football, tennis or golf?

120. In which country did Mike Reid die in 2007 – Germany, Spain or France?

Wendy Richard

121. What was Wendy Richard's birth surname – Emmerson, Emerton or Eaton?

122. Name the programme, with a theme tune played by Acker Bilk, in which Wendy made her first TV appearance in 1961.

123. Wendy first became familiar to TV audiences playing Joyce Harker in which 1960s BBC soap opera?

124. Which dizzy blonde did Wendy play in Are You Been Served? between 1972 and 1985?

125. Wendy appeared as Private Walker's girlfriend in which British sitcom?

126. Wendy appeared in two 'Carry On' films. Can you name them?

127. Wendy appeared in which sequel to Are You Been Served? in 1992-93?

128. What was the name of Wendy's character in EastEnders?

129. How many times did Wendy marry – 2, 3 or 4?

130. True or false: Wendy's last husband was 20 years her junior?

Pam St Clement

131. Which character does Pam St Clement currently play in EastEnders?

132. In which year did Pam join the cast of EastEnders – 1986, 1987 or 1988?

133. What was the first name of Pam's famous on-screen 'spinning bow tie' husband?

134. True or false: Pam was placed into foster care after her mother died and her father remarried?

135. What was Pam's profession before becoming an actress – policewoman, teacher or nurse?

136. In 1979, Pam appeared in which other soap opera – Neighbours, Emmerdale or Coronation Street?

137. Pam St Clement is a stage name taken from a street in which London Borough – Walford, Islington or Holloway?

138. In which year was Pam born – 1940, 1942 or 1944?

139. True or false: Pam is the longest-serving cast member of EastEnders?

140. What was the surname of Pam's character when she joined EastEnders?

'Dirty Den'

141. In which year did Den first appear in EastEnders – 1995, 1986 or 1987?

142. What is 'Dirty Den's' full name?

143. True or false: Den was originally going to be named Jack?

144. What was the name of Den's dog?

145. Which actress played Den's wife?

146. Name the teenager who became the mother of Den's daughter, Vicky.

147. What was the name of Den's posh mistress?

148. Den was shot by a man carrying a gun concealed in a bunch of what kind of flowers?

149. From which country did Den 'return from the dead'?

150. Who finally killed 'Dirty Den'?

Dawn Swann

151. Dawn Swann is a character in which soap opera?

152. Can you name the actress who plays Dawn Swann?

153. In what year did Dawn arrive on the scene?

154. True or false: Dawn is Mickey Miller's sister?

155. Who is the father of Dawn's daughter, Summer, following a heated love affair?

156. Can you name the doctor who tried to steal Dawn's daughter, Summer?

157. Which two men competed for Dawn's attention?

158. Following on from the previous question, which one did Dawn choose, who subsequently postponed the wedding and was eventually stabbed to death?

159. Who posted a petrol-soaked rag through Dawn's letter box?

160. Where did Garry propose to Dawn by putting an engagement ring on a cocktail stick, only to be turned down?

Phil Mitchell

161. Can you name the actor who plays Phil Mitchell?

162. In which year did Phil arrive in EastEnders' Albert Square – 1998, 1990 or 1992?

163. What is the name of Phil's brother?

164. How many times has Phil been married – 1, 2 or 3?

165. Phil had an affair with his brother's wife. Can you name her?

166. On which road is Phil's garage located, under a railway bridge?

167. What is the name of Phil's partially deaf son?

168. With whom did Phil enter into a marriage of convenience and what country was she from?

169. Phil was stalked by which 'drunken loner' after they met at an Alcoholics Anonymous meeting?

170. True or false: Phil is the second-longest-running male character to appear in EastEnders?

William Roache

171. William Roache is best known for his role as Ken Barlow in which soap opera?

172. In which did William first appear as Ken Barlow – 1960, 1961 or 1962?

173. True or false: William is the only remaining member of the original cast?

174. In which year was William born – 1922, 1932 or 1942?

175. What is William's middle name – Peter, Paul or Patrick?

176. True or false: William was declared bankrupt in 1999?

177. In 1999 William was the recipient of which British Soap Award?

178. William is a strong supporter of which political party?

179. What number is William's on-screen residence in Coronation Street?

180. What was William's on-screen profession?

John Savident

181. John is best known for playing the character Fred Elliot in which soap opera?

182. In which year was John born – 1928, 1938 or 1948?

183. On which of the Channel Islands was John born – Guernsey, Jersey or Alderney?

184. What was John's career before becoming an actor – policeman, fireman or nurse?

185. John played a part in which satirical science-fiction film based on a novel by Anthony Burgess and directed by Stanley Kubrick?

186. In which year did John make his TV debut – 1966, 1968 or 1970?

187. What was the occupation of John's character in Coronation Street?

188. True or false: John was stabbed in the neck by a man he met at Manchester's gay village?

189. In which year did John leave Coronation Street – 2003, 2004 or 2005?

190. Following on from the previous question, how did John's character, Fred, die?

Elizabeth (Liz) Dawn

191. In which year was Elizabeth born – 1938, 1939 or 1940?

192. What was Elizabeth's name at birth – Silvia Butterworth, Silvia Butterfield or Silvia Butterwood?

193. Where in Yorkshire was Elizabeth born – Leeds, Bradford or Halifax?

194. Elizabeth is best known for her role in which soap opera?

195. Following on from the previous question, what character did she play?

196. True or false: Elizabeth was one of the alien voices in the Cadbury's smash advert in the 1970s?

197. In 2000 Elizabeth was chosen as the Lady Mayoress of which city – Sheffield, Leeds or York?

198. Which of the following honours did Elizabeth receive in 2000 – MBE, OBE or Dame?

199. In what year did Elizabeth's character make her final appearance after 33 years?

200. What was the name of Elizabeth's on-screen husband?

Julie Goodyear

201. Julie was born in which English county – Yorkshire, Lancashire or Essex?

202. In which decade was Julie born – 1930s, 1940s or 1950s?

203. What was Julie's surname at birth – Kemp, Kent or Keen?

204. Julie received which honour from the Queen in 1996 – MBE, OBE or Dame?

205. What is the title of Julie's autobiography – Just Julie, Just Me or Just My Life?

206. True or false: Julie was given just a year to live between 1979 and 1980?

207. In 2006, in which other soap opera did Julie have a brief role as Mrs Temple, who owned a B&B – Hollyoaks, Neighbours or Home and Away?

208. Julie appeared in Celebrity Stars in Their Eyes, performing as whom – Marlene Dietrich, Marilyn Munroe or Betty Davis?

209. Julie appeared in a commercial for which breakfast cereal – Shredded Wheat, Wheetabix or Kellogg's Cornflakes?

210. How much weight did Julie loose in Celebrity Fit Club – 1 stone 10 pounds, 2 stone or none at all?

Elsie Tanner

211. Elsie Tanner was a character in which soap opera?

212. Can you name the actress who played Elsie Tanner?

213. True or false: Elsie Tanner appeared in the very first episode of this soap?

214. In which year was Elsie Tanner's final appearance in the show – 1984, 1985 or 1986?

215. Following on from the previous question, Elsie emi grated to which country – Spain, Portugal or Ireland?

216. True or false: former Prime Minister James Callaghan described Elsie Tanner as 'the sexiest thing on television'?

217. What was the name of Elsie's first husband?

218. Elsie first worked in which department store – LA Modes, Miami Modes or Vegas Modes?

219. Elsie flirted on and off for many years with which screen character – Len Fairclough, Jack Duckworth or Brian Clough?

220. True or false: Elsie Tanner was the first ever character seen on UK television eating a strawberry sorbet?

Mike Baldwin

221. Which actor played Mike Baldwin in Coronation Street?

222. In which year did Mike make his first appearance in the soap – 1972, 1974 or 1976?

223. Who was Mike's sworn enemy?

224. Mike had numerous relationships and wives, resulting in how many sons – 2, 3 or 4?

225. Following on from the previous question, Mike was involved with which two Barlow women, and which one had a son by him?

226. What was Mike's business called – Underworld, Underwear or Underworn?

227. Mike realised that he still loved which one of his ex-wives as she lay on her deathbed?

228. Mike was diagnosed with Alzheimer's Disease at the age of 63, but what caused his death at the age of 64 outside his factory?

229. Mike died in the arms of his arch-enemy, Ken Barlow, uttering which words to him before he slipped away – (A) 'You're finished Barlow, Deirdre loves me, she's mine', (B) 'You're finished Barlow, you can't exist without me' or (C) 'You're finished Barlow, I know something you don't'?

230. In which year was Mike's last episode aired – 2005, 2006 or 2007?

Bet Lynch

231. Bet Lynch was a character in which soap opera?

232. Can you name the actress who played Bet Lynch?

233. In which year did Bet Lynch first appear in the soap – 1964, 1966 or 1968?

234. In 1970, Bet worked as a barmaid in the Rovers Return Inn under which landlady – Betty Turpin, Ena Sharples or Annie Walker?

235. True or false: Bet became Newton and Ridley's first unmarried landlady in 1985?

236. In 1987, Bet Lynch married which character – Alec Gilroy, Len Fairclough or Ray Langton?

237. Following on from the previous question, in which year did Bet's marriage end – 1988, 1990 or 1992?

238. Which couple succeeded Bet as the new owners of the Rovers?

239. In 2003, whom did Bet help escape from prison in Blackpool?

240. One of Bet's defining attributes was the many outfits she wore designed from which cat-skin print – cheetah, tiger or leopard?

Patrick Mower

241. Patrick Mower plays Rodney Blackstock in which soap opera?

242. In which year is Patrick believed to have been born – 1940, 1950 or 1960?

243. What is Patrick's middle name – Andrew, Archibald or Adrian?

244. Patrick is believed to have been born in which university city – Cambridge, Durham or Oxford?

245. Patrick trained as an engineering draughtsman at which UK vehicle company based at Longbridge in the 1950s and 1960s – Leyland, BMC or Austin Morris?

246. True or false: the marriage of Patrick's parents was thought to have been bigamous and his birth was never registered?

247. Later on in his life, Patrick discovered that he might have been born in which part of South Wales – Pontypridd, Pentrebach or Pantygraigwen?

248. Patrick featured in which 'Carry On' film – Carry On Matron, Carry On England or Carry On Cowboy?

249. Patrick appeared in which 1973 'special' police drama alongside George Sewell?

250. What is the title of Patrick's autobiography – My Story, My Way or My Life?

Ronald Magill

251. Ronald Magill is best remembered for playing Amos Brearly in which soap opera?

252. Ronald was born in 1920 in which city located in the East Riding of Yorkshire that has cream-coloured tele phone boxes?

253. True or false: from the age of nine, Ronald grew up in an orphanage in Birmingham?

254. During World War II, Ronald served in which corps – Royal Signals, The Rifles or Queen's Division?

255. Ronald joined the soap when it was first aired in which year – 1970, 1971 or 1972?

256. Ronald teamed up behind the bar of the Woolpack Inn with which other character?

257. In 1970, Ronald appeared alongside Charlton Heston, Jason Robards and John Gielgud in which film – Ben Hur, Julius Caesar or Planet of the Apes?

258. Ronald became famous for which distinguishing facial feature?

259. Following on from the previous question, on which show did he shave this feature off – Wogan, Parkinson or The Late Late Show?

260. Which Sugden did Ronald's character marry before his final appearance in 1995?

Elizabeth Estensen

261. In which soap opera dose Elizabeth play the role of Diane Sugden?

262. Elizabeth was born in the summer of which year – 1947, 1948 or 1949?

263. Elizabeth's regional roots make her a what – Scouser, Geordie or Brummie?

264. Elizabeth rose to prominence in the 1970s playing the character of Carol Boswell in which Liverpool-based sitcom?

265. Following on from the previous question, which actress did Elizabeth replace in the role – Polly James, Pauline Collins or Nerys Hughes?

266. Which witch-like character did Elizabeth play in a children's ITV programme from the mid-1980s to 1990 – Hand-Bag, Sugar-Bag or T-Bag?

267. In which other soap opera did Elizabeth play the role of Pam Middleton between 1996 and 1998?

268. In Emmerdale, with which shady character did Elizabeth have a dalliance while married to her on- screen husband, Jack?

269. True or false: Elizabeth won a Spectacular Scene of the Year award?

270. In which year did Elizabeth join the cast of Emmerdale – 1997, 1998 or 1999?

Lucy Pargeter

271. Lucy appears in Emmerdale playing which character?

272. In which year was Lucy born – 1975, 1977 or 1979?

273. In which county was Lucy born – Derbyshire, Nottinghamshire or Staffordshire?

274. In which year was Lucy's first appearance in Emmerdale – 2000, 2001 or 2002?

275. In which other soap opera did Lucy appear, as stripper Helen Raven?

276. True or false: Lucy is related to ex-EastEnders actress, Alison Pargeter?

277. Lucy was a member of which band that toured with Boyzone in the early 1990s – Paper Dolls, Paper Chase or Paper Trail?

278. Can you name the actress who is Lucy's best friend on set and who plays Katie Sugden?

279. Lucy played the role of Brenda in which 2002 film – Anita and Him, Anita and Me or Anita and Us?

280. At what age did Lucy sign up with a showbiz agent – 16, 17 or 18?

Jack Sugden

281. Which actor originally portrayed Jack Sugden in Emmerdale Farm between 1972 and 1976?

282. What was Jack's occupation?

283. In the story, Jack left home in 1964 and then returned after his father's death from which major city?

284. Jack moved away again in 1976. Where did he go?

285. Which actor played Jack Sugden on his return to Emmerdale in 1980?

286. During the four years that he was away Jack wrote a book, giving it what title?

287. How many times has Jack been married – 1, 2 or 3?

288. What are the names of his biological son and daughter?

289. Who accidentally shot Jack in an act of revenge?

290. In which country did Jack die?

Jasmine Thomas

291. Jasmine Thomas is a character in which soap opera?

292. Which actress plays Jasmine Thomas – Meg Johnson, Jenna-Louise Coleman or Anne Charleston?

293. In which year did Jasmine first appear on our screens – 2003, 2005 or 2007?

294. Jasmine moved in with her uncle, who goes by the name of what?

295. Jasmine was a journalist with which local paper – Hotton Courier, Emmerdale Times or Sutton Courier?

296. Continuing from the previous question, Jasmine was set the task of finding who's murderer?

297. Which character stole Jasmine's boyfriend, David Metcalf, when she returned to the village?

298. Whom did Jasmine kill with a chair leg?

299. Following on from the previous question, which two characters helped Jasmine dump the body in the lake?

300. Following the murder, Jasmine went into hiding with her granddad in which country – Ireland, Scotland or Wales?

Zak Dingle

301. In which soap opera does Zak Dingle feature?

302. In which year did Zak Dingle appear on the scene – 1992, 1993 or 1994?

303. In which year was Zak born – 1951, 1952 or 1953?

304. What is the name of Zak's home – Well Wisher's Cottage, Wishing Well Cottage or Wisher's Well Cottage?

305. What is the first name of Zak's wife?

306. Which actor plays Zak Dingle?

307. Zak disappeared from Emmerdale to find the family fortune in which country – Cuba, Chile or Colombia?

308. Zak is famous for which type of fighting?

309. What are the names of Zak's two dead sons?

310. True or false: Zak was embarrassingly knocked out by Mandy Dingle before a comeback fight?

Chris Fountain

311. Chris best known for appearing in which teen soap?

312. Following on from the previous question, which character does Chris play – Justin Burton, Richard Burton or Barry Burton?

313. Chris has played his soap role since which year – 2001, 2002 or 2003?

314. What is Chris Fountain's middle name – Ronan, Ryan or Ronald?

315. Chris was a runner up in the 3rd. series of which ITV dancing show?

316. In which two other dramas has Chris appeared, one set in the village of Skelthwaite and the other in a hospital near Aidensfield?

317. Chris took part in the BBC show Just the Two of Us. Can you name his former S Club 7 singing partner?

318. Whom has Chris referred to as his dream girl – Lydia Waters, Paris Hilton or Jessica Fox?

319. True or false: Chris planned to pursue a professional ice hockey career?

320. Which football team dose Chris support – Bradford City, Leeds United or Huddersfield Town?

John Pickard

321. John is a British actor who currently appears in Hollyoaks as which character?

322. In which year did John join the cast of Hollyoaks – 2002, 2005 or 2007?

323. What is the occupation of John's character in Hollyoaks?

324. John's brother, Nick, also appears in Hollyoaks, playing which character?

325. True or false: John and Nick are on-screen brothers?

326. How many years after Nick did John join Hollyoaks – 5, 10 or 15?

327. In which other soap opera did John appear between 1993 and 1996?

328. John appeared in Grange Hill between 1990 and 1991, playing which character – Neil Timpson, Peter 'Tucker' Jenkins or Benny Green?

329. True or false: John disliked Jeremy Beadle?

330. Which of the following football teams does John support – Manchester United, Chelsea or Tottenham Hotspur?

Sarah Jayne Dunn

331. Sarah Jayne Dunn is an actress on which British soap opera?

332. Which soap opera character does Sarah play – Mandy Richardson, Cindy Cunningham or Sarah Barnes?

333. Following on from the previous question, in which year did Sarah first appear as her character – 1992, 1994 or 1996?

334. Following on from the previous question, in which year did she last appear as her character – 2002, 2004 or 2006?

335. In which BBC daytime soap did Sarah appear?

336. In which year was Sarah born – 1979, 1980 or 1981?

337. In 2000, Sarah returned to Hollyoaks for the funeral of which character played by Ali Bastian?

338. In 2008, Sarah had a brief role as Maroni's mistress in which film starring Batman and The Joker?

339. In 2009, Sarah co-starred with Dannii Minogue in which British spy film – Vauxhall Crossed, Lambeth Crossed or Charing Crossed?

340. True or false: Jane is the daughter of Clive Dunn of Dad's Army fame?

Samantha Giles

341. Samantha's latest soap opera appearance has been in Hollyoaks, playing which character?

342. Which past EastEnders actress, who played Lorraine Wicks, did Samantha take over from in Hollyoaks?

343. In which soap opera did Samantha play Bernice Thomas?

344. Name two other soap operas in which Samantha has appeared.

345. In which long-running ITV series set in a Yorkshire village did Samantha have a starring role?

346. Following on from the previous question, can you name the character she played?

347. Samantha's first break was a play directed by which iconic EastEnders Bible-quoting actress?

348. True or false: Samantha has performed Tarot readings in London's Covent Garden?

349. Samantha picked up a best actress award for her role in Emmerdale from which TV magazine – TV Quick, What's On TV or TV Times?

350. For the time being (2009), to which country has Samantha's Hollyoaks character moved?

Tony Hutchinson

351. True or false: Tony Hutchinson is a character in Coronation Street?

352. Can you name the actor who plays Tony Hutchinson – Nick Pickard, James McKenna or Jack Osborne?

353. Tony is the only original character still on the show since the soap opera first started in which year – 1993, 1994 or 1995?

354. What is Tony Hutchinson's occupation?

355. Tony had a brief departure, driving off with whom in the car?

356. Tony returned, wanting to make contact with his son, whose name is – William, Edward or Harry?

357. Tony briefly dated which bisexual woman?

358. Tony decided to run for council, but who defeated him?

359. Can you name Tony and Mandy's daughter who died?

360. What is the name of Tony's brother?

Steph Cunningham

361. Steph Cunningham is a character in which soap opera?

362. Which actress plays Steph Cunningham?

363. In which year was Steph's first appearance in the soap – 2000, 2001 or 2002?

364. What is Steph's stage name?

365. True or false: Steph is consecutively the longest-running female character?

366. From what medical condition does Steph suffer?

367. Steph was left what inheritance by her great-auntie Reenie – a horse, a pony or a donkey?

368. On what day was Steph widowed?

369. How did Steph's husband, Max, die?

370. Steph was left to look after Tom, who is what relation to Tom – father, son or brother?

Darren Osborne

371. Darren Osborne is a character in which soap opera?

372. Who was the first actor to portray Darren?

373. Who currently plays Darren?

374. Darren returned from America to live with his father, Jack, in which pub?

375. Darren left to go back to America for how many years – 2, 3 or 4?

376. In 2006, Darren valiantly tried to fight a fire at the pub, which was started by whom?

377. What addiction caused Darren more and more pain – drugs, gambling or alcohol?

378. True or false: Darren was shot outside the pub in a hostage crisis?

379. Along with his father, Jack, Darren received a prison sentence of how many months – 10, 20 or 30?

380. On Darren's return from prison, what became his occupation in The Dog in the Pond pub – barman, cellarman or toilet cleaner?

Jason Donavan

381. What was the name of Jason's character in Neighbours?

382. What is Jason's middle name?

383. In which year was Jason born – 1966, 1968 or 1970?

384. True or false: Jason is the son of a well-known actor?

385. In Neighbours, which actress played Jason's on-screen wife?

386. Following on from the previous question, Jason and this actress/singer had a chart hit with a duet in 1989. Can you name the song?

387. True or false: in the past Jason suffered from a serious drug problem?

388. Which 'colourful' character did Jason play in a stage show?

389. In 2006, Jason finished third in which celebrity reality TV programme?

390. In 2008, Jason played the character of Daniel Marrack in which soap opera set in Cornwall?

Alan Dale

391. Alan Dale played which Robinson character in Neighbours between 1985 and 1993?

392. In which country was Alan born – Canada, Australia or New Zealand?

393. What sport did Alan play before becoming an actor – football, rugby or cricket?

394. Alan moved to Australia where he was cast as Dr John Forrest in which Australian soap opera?

395. Alan went to which country to revitalise his career after leaving Neighbours?

396. True or false: Alan's wife, Tracy Pearson, is a former Miss Australia?

397. Can you name the role that Alan played for seven episodes of the second season of TV series 24?

398. Alan's son, Simon, is a radio announcer on which radio station – Heart, Magic or Kiss 100?

399. Who is Alan's acting hero – Sean Connery, Marlon Brando or Gene Hackman?

400. What caused the death of Alan's character, Jim Robinson, in Neighbours?

Kylie Minogue

401. Which character did Kylie play when she joined Neighbours?

402. In which year did Kylie join Neighbours – 1986, 1987 or 1988?

403. In 2008, Kylie was given which order by Queen Elizabeth 11 – CBE, MBE or OBE?

404. Which songwriters and producers did Kylie sign for between 1988 and 1992?

405. What was Kylie's first UK hit?

406. In Australia, which song rendition launched Kylie's singing career?

407. Name the tour that Kylie resumed in 2006 after recovering from breast cancer.

408. True or false: Kylie is half Welsh?

409. Kylie was the voice of which character in The Magic Roundabout?

410. What is the title of Kylie's book, published in 2002?

Holly Valance

411. In which Australian soap did Holly portray Felicity Scully between 1999 and 2002?

412. In which year was Holly born in Melbourne, Australia – 1983, 1984 or 1985?

413. What is Holly's Serbian birth surname – Vaduka, Vukadinovic or Vudanicovic?

414. True or false: Harry Hill's cousin was Holly's grandfather?

415. Holly left Neighbours to pursue a career in which industry?

416. What was Holly's teen career before being discovered as an actress for Neighbours?

417. What was the title of Holly's first single, which debuted at number one in the UK singles chart – 'Cheek to Cheek', 'Kiss Kiss' or 'Love is Love'?

418. What was Holly's debut album called – Headprints, Footprints or Fingerprints?

419. In which year did Holly return to acting – 2004, 2005 or 2006?

420. In 2008, Holly played the role of a singer in which film alongside Liam Neeson?

Paul Robinson

421. Paul Robinson is a character in which soap opera?

422. Which actor plays Paul Robinson?

423. In which year did Paul first appear in Neighbours – 1984, 1985 or 1986?

424. True or false: one of Paul's nicknames is 'Stumpy'?

425. Paul was likened to which Dallas character?

426. Paul dropped out of university to become which of the following – an airline steward, a check-in assistant or a pilot?

427. In 1992, Paul left to run Lassiter's Hotel in which country?

428. In which year did Paul return to Ramsay Street – 2002, 2004 or 2006?

429. Who attempted to strangle Paul?

430. How many times has Paul been shot – 1, 2 or 3?

Madge Bishop

431. In which soap opera was Madge Bishop a character?

432. Can you name the actress who portrayed Madge Bishop and is now in Emmerdale?

433. In which year did Madge first appear – 1984, 1986 or 1988?

434. For how many years was Madge on the show – 11, 12 or 13?

435. Madge remained at the same address on Ramsay Street, but what was the number of the house?

436. Following on from the previous question, what was the name of Madge's brother who previously owned the property?

437. Madge had a daughter played by which famous singer?

438. In 1987 Madge got married for the second time, to which character?

439. What was the name of Madge's first husband?

440. In 2001 Madge died, but what was the cause of her death?

Karl Kennedy

441. Karl Kennedy is a character in which Australian soap opera?

442. Which actor plays Karl Kennedy – Alan Fletcher, Alan Dale or Alan Coleman?

443. In which year did Karl Kennedy appear on the scene – 1992, 1993 or 1994?

444. What is Karl's occupation – handyman, taxi driver or doctor?

445. True or false: Karl's middle name is Rupert?

446. Karl was named after which Communist revolutionary icon?

447. Where did Karl propose to his ex-wife, Susan, for the second time – London, Paris or New York?

448. Which Spice Girl found Karl's engagement ring?

449. Name Karl's university band – The Wrong Prescription, The Right Prescription or The Left Prescription?

450. True or false: in 1987 the actor who played Karl Kennedy appeared as a mechanic in Neighbours?

Dannii Minogue

451. Dannii appeared in Home and Away between 1989 and 1990 as which character?

452. What was the title of Dannii's debut single – Love and Kisses, This Is It or All I Wanna Do?

453. Before Home and Away, Dannii appeared in which Australian soap that ran from 1976 to 1983 and focused on a family during World War II?

454. Is Dannii younger or older than her sister?

455. On which talent show was Dannii a judge and mentor alongside Simon Cowell?

456. True or false: following on from the previous question, Dannii was responsible for the departure of Sharon Osbourne?

457. True or false: Dannii posed nude in Playboy magazine after her divorce from Julian McMahon and it became one of the best-selling editions?

458. To which Formula One driver did Dannii become engaged – Jensen Button, Michael Schumacher or Jacques Villeneuve?

459. In 1997, which UK music programme did Dannii host?

460. True or false: in 2002, the British National Party (BNP) claimed that Dannii supported their cause?

Heath Ledger

461. Heath guest-starred in Home and Away, but what was the name of his character – Scott Robinson, Scott Irwin or Scott Robin?

462. In which year did Heath appear in Home and Away – 1996, 1997 or 1998?

463. Heath was an avid player of which board game – Chess, Backgammon or Monopoly?

464. What was Heath's middle name – Anton, Andrew or Aspin?

465. In which city in Western Australia was Heath born?

466. In which year was Heath born – 1979, 1980 or 1981?

467. In how many films did Heath appear – 17, 18 or 19?

468. Heath portrayed a gay cowboy in which controversial film?

469. Can you name the film in which Heath played The Joker?

470. What was Heath Ledger's age at the time of his death – 27, 28 or 29?

Lynne McGranger

471. Lynne McGranger plays the role of Irene Roberts in which soap opera?

472. In which year was Lynne born – 1951, 1952 or 1953?

473. Lynne started out as a primary school teacher and trained at an advanced educational centre in which part of New South Wales – Hagga Hagga, Wagga Wagga or Kagga Kagga?

474. In her early years, Lynne had a small part in which medical series based in the fictional outback town of Cooper's Crossing and starring Andrew McFarlane?

475. In which year was Lynne made a permanent cast member of Home and Away – 1992, 1993 or 1994?

476. In which show does Lynne appear every Friday at 10.00 a.m. – Morning Talk Show, The Morning Show or Good Morning Australia?

477. What is the occupation of Lynne's character in Home and Away?

478. Who played Irene Roberts before Lynne – Jacqui Phillips, Kate Bell or Jaclyn Albergoni?

479. Who is Lynne's favourite actor – Al Pacino, Robert De Niro or Daniel Craig?

480. What is Lynne's natural hair colour?

Naomi Watts

481. In which Australian soap opera did Naomi Watts appear?

482. Following on from the previous question, can you name the character she played and in what year?

483. True or false: Naomi's mother is Welsh?

484. Naomi's father was a road manager with which band, whose hit albums included, amongst others, The Wall and The Dark Side of the Moon?

485. True or false: Naomi was born in Australia?

486. In the United States Naomi landed her first supporting role in which film – Tank Girl, Jet Girl or Rocket Girl?

487. Naomi starred in her most commercially successful film, King Kong, in 2005, playing which character?

488. Naomi had wanted to be an actress ever since watching which film – Fame, Saturday Night Fever or Grease?

489. In which country was Naomi a model – Thailand, Japan or Hong Kong?

490. Who is the father of Naomi's two sons – Heath Ledger, Stephen Hopkins or Liev Schreiber?

Colleen Smart

491. Colleen Smart is a fictional character in which Australian soap opera?

492. Which actress portrays Colleen Smart – Lyn Collingwood, Christie Hayes or Charlotte Best?

493. In which year did Colleen become a regular character – 1999, 2000 or 2001?

494. What is Colleen's occupation?

495. Name Colleen's sister, whom she found out about from a diary contained in an unearthed time capsule?

496. Who held Colleen as a hostage in the Summer Bay house?

497. By what nickname is busybody Colleen known – Long Beak, Sticky Beak or Nosey Beak?

498. Which pageant did Colleen reintroduce to Summer Bay in 2005, which she regularly boasts about winning in the past – Miss Pinch, Miss Squeeze or Miss Groper?

499. True or false: Colleen became a Stewart as a result of her mother's infidelity with Alf and Morag Stewart's father?

500. True or false: Colleen dreamt of being a Stewart when she was growing up?

Alfred 'Alf' Stewart

501. What is Alf's occupation in Home and Away?

502. What is the name of the actor who plays Alf?

503. In which year did Alf make his first appearance – 1986, 1987 or 1988?

504. What is Alf's middle name – Douglas, Daniel or Dougal?

505. What were the names of Alf's two wives?

506. How did Alf's first wife die?

507. In which year did Alf's second wife die – 1999, 2000 or 2001?

508. Apart from, 'Alf', what is Alfred's other nickname given by Vinnie Patterson who is the father of Vincent junior, 'V J' Patterson?

509. Who dated Alf, but was secretly after his money and was eventually arrested after being caught out by Rachel Armstrong?

510. What is the name of Alf's deceased son?

Aden Jefferies

511. Aden Jefferies is a fictional character in which Australian soap opera?

512. Can you name the actor who portrays Aden Jefferies?

513. What is Aden's occupation?

514. Aden was born in Summer Bay, but who eventually brought him up?

515. Aden has two older brothers. Can you name them?

516. Aden lives with Nicole and Roman, who are known as which family?

517. In which year did Aden first appear at Summer Bay High School – 2003, 2004 or 2005?

518. Aden decided not to attend university because he wanted to stay in Summer Bay to look after whom?

519. Who ruined Aden's first application to work on the fishing boat?

520. Can you name Aden's fellow worker who was raped by Robbo?

Christopher Timothy

521. In which daytime soap opera did Christopher appear?

522. Following on from the previous question, which character did Christopher play?

523. In which year was Christopher born – 1940, 1942 or 1944?

524. What is Christopher's nationality – Welsh, English or Irish?

525. Christopher played the well-known role of James Herriot in which 1970s and 1980s TV serial?

526. What was Christopher's occupation as James Herriot?

527. In 2005 Christopher appeared in Casualty as the murderer of which long-standing character?

528. True or false: Christopher's father was a BBC announcer?

529. Christopher appeared in Holby City as which character – Paul Collins, Phil Collins or Chris Collins?

530. In 1971 Christopher appeared as a character called George Swainson in which police drama?

Matt Kennard

531. Matt Kennard portrays Archie Hallam in which BBC medical drama?

532. In which year did Matt start playing the role of Archie Hallam – 2005, 2006 or 2007?

533. Between 2000 and 2003 Matt appeared in Coronation Street as which character – Joe Carter, Jimmy Mullins or Curly Watts?

534. In 2006, Matt appeared in which police drama as PC Kevin Sharpe – The Thin Blue Line, The Bill or Holby Blue?

535. Which Manchester United football player did Matt portray in the dramatisation of the 1958 Munich air disaster – Duncan Edwards, Bobby Charlton or Harry Greg?

536. Can you name Matt's twin brother who is also an actor?

537. In 2001 Matt portrayed Gareth North in which police series set in 1960s Yorkshire?

538. In which year was Matt born – 1982, 1983 or 1984?

539. In which seaport on the Humber Estuary famous for its fish was Matt born?

540. What is Matt's occupation as Archie Hallam?

Angela Lonsdale

541. Angela currently appears in Doctors as which character – doctor, paramedic or policewoman?

542. What is the name Angela's character in Doctors?

543. In which year did Angela join the cast of Doctors – 2006, 2007 or 2008?

544. True or false: Angela, who originates from the Lake District, appeared in the TV series The Lakes?

545. Angela played a police officer in Coronation Street, but what was the name of her character?

546. Who was Angela's on-screen husband in Coronation Street?

547. Angela is married to which Mitchell from EastEnders – Phil, Billy or Grant?

548. Angela played another policewoman in which wintry-sounding ITV police drama?

549. In Casualty Angela played a character called Karen, but what was her surname – Gateshead, Sunderland or Washington?

550. True or false: Angela played a police officer in The Bill?

Emma Samms

551. In 2005 Emma portrayed Amanda Clay in which medical drama?

552. Following on from the previous question, who was Amanda's husband?

553. In which year was Emma born – 1960, 1961 or 1962?

554. What is Emma's birth surname – Samuel, Samuelson or Samson?

555. Emma trained as a ballet dancer but had to quit at the age of 15 due to an injury to which part of her body – foot, leg or hip?

556. Emma portrayed Holly Sutton Scorpio in which American medical soap opera?

557. Emma played the role of Fallon Carrington Colby in which 1980s prime-time American soap opera along side Joan Collins?

558. Following on from the previous question, in which spin-off, starring Charlton Heston, did Emma become a main character alongside Emmerdale's Maxwell Caulfield?

559. In 2003 Emma had a run in which spin-off medical drama of Casualty?

560. In 2007 in which police drama did Emma portray drug addict, Ella Winstanley?

Adrian Lewis Morgan

561. Adrian appears on the BBC daytime soap Doctors, playing which character?

562. Adrian's character in Doctors is an associate at The Mill, but what is his occupation in Leatherbridge?

563. In which year was Adrian born – 1969, 1971 or 1973?

564. True or false: Adrian is Irish?

565. In which other TV medical drama has Adrian appeared?

566. Following on from the previous question, what was the name of his character?

567. What was the name of Adrian's character in the rock opera Rent – Roger, Ronnie or Rupert?

568. What is Adrian's favourite film – 12 Angry Men, 12 Angry Months or 12 Angry Viewers?

569. Adrian played the role of Marius in which West End theatre production?

570. In which year did Adrian join the cast of Doctors – 2004, 2005 or 2006?

Diane Keen

571. Diane portrays Julia Parsons in which medical drama?

572. Diane was born in London in which year – 1936, 1946 or 1956?

573. In her early career Diane appeared nude in which 1973 British sex comedy – The Sex Fiend, The Sex Thief or The Sex Catcher?

574. In 1972 Diane portrayed the receptionist at the Feathers Hotel Connelton in which British country soap opera?

575. Diane appeared in which long-running series of coffee advertisements – Nesquick, Nescafé or Nestlé?

576. Diane had a role in which Liverpool-based former soap opera?

577. In 1978 and 1980 Diane appeared as Laura Dickens, alongside Roy Marsden, in which spy drama set around the Cold War and espionage?

578. Diane became a regular in which Ruth Rendell mystery, portraying the wife of Inspector Burden?

579. True or false: Diane was second choice to play Dr Styles in Doctor Who – Resurrection of the Darleks?

580. What is the name of Diane's ex-husband, who appeared in Doctors in 2004 for one episode as Alan Cordery – Ron Greenwood, Paul Greenwood or John Greenwood?

Anita Carey

581. Anita currently appears in Doctors, playing which character?

582. What is the occupation of Anita's character in Doctors?

583. True or false: Anita's character in Doctors in an ex-matron?

584. Anita appeared in which other medical drama for one episode as Kaye Skinner – Casualty, Holby City or Flying Doctors?

585. Until recently Anita was best known as Joyce Smedley in which soap opera?

586. In the 1970s Anita appeared in two police dramas. One of them was Z Cars, but what was the other one, starring Jack Warner?

587. Anita appeared in which 1998 comedy film – Still Crazy, Still Mad or Still Raving?

588. Anita had a small role as a voice actor playing Venant in which PlayStation game?

589. True or false: Anita is related to Jim Carrey?

590. Who is Anita's hero – Elvis, John F. Kennedy or Bob Dylan?

Simon MacCorkindale

591. Simon portrayed Harry Harper in which medical drama?

592. In which year did Harry Harper arrive on our screens –
2002, 2003 or 2004?

593. In which year was Harry's last appearance, although the
role was left open in case Simon wanted to return – 2007,
2008 or 2009?

594. Simon initially planned to join the RAF, but failed the
medical on what grounds – physical fitness, flat feet or
eyesight test?

595. Simon starred alongside Jane Wyman in which 1980s and
1990s American prime-time soap opera set around the
Channing family, in which he portrayed Greg Reardon?

596. Simon was born in Ely, Cambridgeshire, in which year –
1942, 1952 or 1962?

597. Can you name Simon's first wife, who starred as KGB spy,
Pola Ivanova, in James Bond's A View to a Kill?

598. Can you name Simon's second wife, who appeared in
EastEnders in 2001 as Margaret Walker and dated singer
Jack Jones and Prince Charles?

599. Where did Simon marry his second wife – Vanuatu, Tonga
or Fiji?

600. In 1977 Simon joined Robert Powell in which religious TV
mini-series as Lucius?

Charles Dale

601. Charles plays a porter in which medical drama?

602. Following on from the previous question, the porter is named after which McDonald's product?

603. What is Charles' nationality – Welsh, Irish or English?

604. Charles got his big break in TV as, Gary 'Chef ' Alcock, in which 'watery' soap?

605. Between 2000 and 2002 Charles played Dennis Stringer in which soap opera?

606. Charles starred as Clive, one of three brothers, in which show that was originally called Paradise Heights?

607. How many times has Charles appeared in Casualty – 1, 2 or 3?

608. Charles appeared as Barney Scott, alongside Robson Green, in which 'spacey' drama?

609. True or false: following on from question 605, Charles' character Dennis Stringer died while driving Les Battersby to hospital?

610. Charles was born in which year of 'The Big Freeze' – 1962, 1963 or 1964?

Caroline Langrishe

611. Caroline portrays executive director Marilyn Fox in which medical drama?

612. What were Caroline's first words as Marilyn: (A) 'Who's the prat that talked to the press?', (B) 'Have you been talking to the press?' or (C) 'Who the hell's been talking to the press?'

613. Caroline was born in London in which year – 1956, 1957 or 1958?

614. In 1990 Caroline appeared in several episodes of which ITV series alongside Clive Owen – Hitman, Chancer or The Pretenders?

615. Caroline is probably best known for her role as Charlotte Cavendish in which BBC drama series set around an antiques dealer played by Ian McShane?

616. In 1996 and 1997 Caroline played Lady Anne Camoynes in which TV series set around the Napoleonic wars and starring Sean Bean?

617. Caroline portrayed Georgina Channing alongside an ex-Professionals star in which legal drama?

618. Caroline was married to which actor who played the shopkeeper, John O'Leary, in the comedy Father Ted?

619. In 1978 Caroline's first big part was Cosette in which British adaptation of a Victor Hugo novel set in the time of Napoleon's final defeat and featuring Jean Valjean?

620. In 1990 Caroline portrayed Perditia Flaxton-Green in which police drama – Holby Blue, The Bill or Taggart?

Leanne Wilson

621. Leanne is best known for playing a nurse called Claire Guildford in which medical drama?

622. In which other medical drama has Leanne appeared, as Candy Williams?

623. In which American sci-fi series did Leanne appear as Jess, alongside Adrian Paul Hewett of Highlander fame – Tracker, Stargate SG-1 or Battlestar Galactica?

624. True or false: Leanne once posed in men's magazine Maxim?

625. In 2005 Leanne featured in FHM's 100 Sexiest Women in the World listing, being voted into what place – 50th, 60th or 70th?

626. In 2006 Leanne played Nancy Myers in which film, starring alongside Kate Winslet and Jude Law?

627. Leanne appeared in which celebrity game show that was a spin-off of Top Gear?

628. In the BBC TV series New Tricks Leanne played the daughter of which ex-Minder star?

629. What is Leanne's favourite animal – dog, cat or horse?

630. What was the occupation of Leanne's husband, Keith Whallett, when they met in Greece – actor, builder or driver?

Charlie Fairhead

631. Charlie Fairhead is a character in which BBC medical drama?

632. Can you name the actor who portrays Charlie Fairhead?

633. In which year did Charlie make his first appearance – 1985, 1986 or 1987?

634. What is Charlie's current occupation – clinical nurse manager, clinical nurse specialist or senior charge nurse?

635. What was the name of Charlie's deceased wife?

636. What is the name of Charlie's son?

637. In 2008 Charlie bought which British classic sports car – MGB, Morgan or Reliant Scimitar?

638. Following on from the previous question, which car did it replace – Mini, Ford Cortina or Morris Traveller?

639. True or false: Charlie appeared in the first ever episodes of Holby City and Holby Blue?

640. Charlie has also appeared in which crossover storyline – Casualty@HolbyCity, Casualty@HolbyBlue or Casualty@CityHospital?

Ruth Winters

641. Ruth Winters is a character in which medical drama?

642. What is Ruth's occupation – junior doctor, nurse or consultant?

643. In which year did Ruth join the medical team she is associated with – 2005, 2006 or 2007?

644. What is the name of the actress who plays Ruth Winters?

645. Ruth had wanted to become a doctor since the age of what – 8, 9 or 10?

646. Which other character joined the show on the same day as Ruth?

647. Ruth had to face some old demons when which patient was brought into casualty – her mother, her estranged father or her long lost sister?

648. What situation led to Ruth attempting suicide?

649. Who found Ruth hanging in her room?

650. Who was Ruth Winters in her past life in Coronation Street?

Josh Griffiths

651. Josh Griffiths was a character in which medical drama?

652. Can you name the actor who portrayed Josh?

653. What was Josh's occupation?

654. What was the name of Josh Griffiths' deceased wife?

655. Can you name Josh's two deceased children?

656. What caused the deaths of Josh's wife and children?

657. True or false: Josh received a long-service medal from Prince Charles?

658. What was the name of the female attacker who stabbed Josh in the neck in the back of an ambulance – Paula, Tara or Laura?

659. Josh left in 2006, but later returned from which country – India, Bangladesh or Pakistan?

660. Who was the Indian woman for whom Josh realised his true feelings – Devika, Sajini or Benazir?

Paul Bradley

661. Paul is best known for playing the role of Nigel Bates in which soap opera?

662. Since 2005 Paul has appeared in Holby City, but can you name his character?

663. In Holby City, what was the first name of Paul's on- screen wife who committed assisted suicide?

664. True or false: Paul's father was a GP?

665. Paul co-leads a folk band as a guitarist and vocalist. What is the name of the group – The Kippers, The Tunas or The Haddocks?

666. In 2002 Paul had a small role as Yehuda in which Roman Polanski film about a Polish Jewish musician?

667. Although Paul is English, what rugby team does he support – Wales, Australia or Ireland?

668. Paul appeared in which 1980s comedy sci-fi series as Chen, alongside Craig Charles who plays Lloyd in Coronation Street?

669. True or false: Paul adopts the same hero as Anita Carey of Doctors fame?

670. In which year was Paul born – 1955, 1957 or 1959?

Robert Powell

671. Robert plays which character in Holby City – Paul Rose, Ric Griffin or Mark Williams?

672. In which year did Robert join Holby City – 2003, 2004 or 2005?

673. Robert was born in Salford in which year – 1942, 1943 or 1944?

674. What is Robert's middle name – Tyrone, Thomas or Terence?

675. Robert is most famous for his title role in which Franco Zeffirelli production, in which he starred alongside Sir Laurence Olivier?

676. Robert played the non-speaking role of Captain Walker in which Ken Russell film featuring Roger Daltrey?

677. Which Pan's People dancer did Robert marry?

678. In 1978 Robert stepped into the leading role as Richard Hannay in the third film version of which John Buchan novel?

679. Robert appeared in which sitcom with Jasper Carrott of game show Golden Balls fame?

680. In 1969 Robert landed his first starring role as Yellow alongside Michael Cain in which film featuring three Minis?

Patsy Kensit

681. Between 2004 and 2006 Patsy played Sadie King in which Yorkshire soap opera?

682. In 2007 Patsy began her role as Faye Morton in which medical drama?

683. In which other medical drama did Patsy make a guest appearance?

684. Patsy was the lead singer in which group – Eighth Wonder, Eighth Prodigy or Eighth Sensation?

685. Following on from the previous question, what was their only top ten hit, produced by The Pet Shop Boys – 'I'm Not Spooked', 'I'm Not Scared' or 'I'm Not Shocked'?

686. Patsy appeared in The Great Gatsby starring Mia Farrow, whom she would later portray in which 1995 biopic?

687. What was the nickname of Patsy's gangster father – Jimmy The Dip, Johnny The Sag or Joe The Bow?

688. True or false: Patsy's second son was named after Ringo Starr?

689. Patsy is divorced from which Oasis brother?

690. Which Kray twin was godfather to Patsy's brother?

Sharon D. Clarke

691. Sharon is well known for portraying Lola Griffin in which medical drama?

692. In which year did Sharon appear as Lola – 2003, 2004 or 2005?

693. On which ward does Lola work?

694. Sharon sat alongside Russell Watson as a judge on which BBC talent show?

695. Sharon is the narrator for which CBBC programme – Tweenies, Boo! or Sesame Street?

696. In 2000 and 2002 Sharon portrayed Rafiki the monkey in which stage play of a Walt Disney picture?

697. Which character did Sharon play in the musical Chicago – Matron Mama Morton, Mary Sunshine or Velma Kelly?

698. Sharon originated the role of Killer Queen in which Ben Elton/Queen musical production?

699. In 1991 Sharon achieved chart success with a song called 'I Want to Give You Devotion', with which band featuring Steve McCutcheon and Damon Rocheford – Nomad, Nofool or Nonuts?

700. What was the title of the episode in which Lola Griffin left Holby City – 'It's a Mad World', 'Mad World' or 'The World is Mad'?

'Abra' Durant

701. 'Abra' Durant is a character in which medical drama?

702. What is Abra's real first name?

703. Which actor, who played Vyvyan Basterd in The Young Ones and Eddie Hitler in Bottom, portrays the character of Abra?

704. In which year did Abra first appear on our screens – 2003, 2005 or 2007?

705. How many times has Abra reappeared – 4, 5 or 6?

706. With which character was Abra romantically involved?

707. Abra fancied which female surgeon, who died after her car collided with a train?

708. Abra performed an illegal transplant with the liver of which animal – cow, pig or goat?

709. What is the first name of Abra's son?

710. 'Abra' is short for the Ghanaian name 'Abrafo', which means – troublemaker, rabble-rouser or firebrand?

Ric Griffin

711. Ric Griffin is a fictional character in which medical drama?

712. Which actor portrays Ric Griffin?

713. What are Ric's two first names – Abina Robert, Aniko Jack or Kobina Eric?

714. In which year did Ric first appear on-screen – 2000, 2001 or 2002?

715. Following on from the previous question, what was the title of the episode – 'Rogue Males', 'Rogue Women' or 'Rogue Doctors'?

716. True or false: Ric is the second longest-serving main character in the show after Chrissie Williams?

717. From which country does Ric originate – Jamaica, Ghana or South Africa?

718. True or false: following on from the previous question, Ric's brother runs a restaurant back in this country?

719. How many times has Ric been married – 1, 3 or 5?

720. What is the name of Ric's dead grandson – Paris Hilton, Paris Khan or Paris Waldorf?

Jayne Grayson

721. Jayne Grayson is a chief executive officer in which medical drama?

722. In which year did Jayne appear in her new role – 2005, 2006 or 2007?

723. What was the title of the episode in which Jayne first appeared – 'Under The Radar', 'The Q Word' or 'Temporary Insanity'?

724. What nationality is Jane?

725. Whom did Jayne replace as chief executive officer – Donald Sutherland, Susan Sutherland or Christopher Sutherland?

726. Jayne appeared in which crossover show?

727. True or false: Jayne ousted her own father from the family business in a hostile takeover?

728. Jayne's husband had an affair with which female surgeon?

729. Jayne urged which bespectacled religious surgeon to do whatever he could to save her son, Christian?

730. What is the name of the actress who plays Jayne Grayson?

Patrick Robinson

731. Which character did Patrick play in Casualty – Charlie Fairhead, Jeff Collier or Martin 'Ash' Ashford?

732. In 2003 Patrick appeared as a CIA agent in the movie Belly of the Beast starring Steven Seagal, but what was the name of his character – Denzil Washington, Leon Washington or George Washington?

733. Patrick played a slave in a play by Simon Schama called Rough Crossings. Can you name the slave, who went on to become a leader in Sierra Leone?

734. Since 2008 Patrick has appeared as Jacob Banks in which police drama?

735. Following on from the previous question, what is the nickname of Patrick's character?

736. True or false: Patrick is the cousin of footballer Emmanuel Eboué?

737. In which year was Patrick born – 1961, 1962 or 1963?

738. Patrick made his stage debut in 1986 in which Shakespeare play – Hamlet, Romeo & Juliet or Macbeth?

739. Which dance routine did Patrick perform with Lisa Maxwell for Comic Relief?

740. What is the occupation of Patrick's on-screen wife, Naomi Woods?

Daniel Flynn

741. What are the rank and name of Daniel's character in The Bill?

742. In which year did Daniel join The Bill – 2005, 2006 or 2007?

743. Daniel's call sign in The Bill is Sierra Oscar – 52, 62 or 72?

744. Daniel has a well-known brother who starred in Soldier, Soldier and had three UK hits with Robson Green. What is his first name?

745. True or false: Daniel's father was a Chinese-born British actor and singer?

746. What is the name Daniel's wife, who starred as Police Sergeant Patricia Dawkins in The Thin Blue Line?

747. True or false: Daniel is a distant relation of actor Errol Flynn?

748. Daniel is said to be a descendent of which 17th century MP who is best known for his involvement in making England a republic and signed King Charles 1 death warrant?

749. Daniel played which character in the film Biggles – Ginger, Strawberry or Blondie?

750. In 1998 Daniel played a criminal in which police drama – The Bill, The Sweeney or The Professionals?

Gina Gold

751. Gina Gold was a character from which police drama?

752. In which year did Gina Gold first appear on-screen – 2002, 2004 or 2006?

753. What was Gina's title – Sergeant, Inspector or Chief Constable?

754. Gina's call sign was Sierra Oscar – 1, 2 or 3?

755. In which year was Gina's last appearance – 2007, 2008 or 2009?

756. What was the reason for Gina's departure – love triangle, killed or retirement?

757. True or false: Gina's husband was PC Dale Smith before they were divorced due to the age gap?

758. Which actress played Gina Gold – Roberta Taylor, Lisa Maxwell or Claire Goose?

759. Gina had an emotional farewell with which Sergeant – Johnny, Smithy or Danny?

760. In which soap opera had Gina starred prior to joining The Bill?

Louisa Lytton

761. Louisa rose to fame in 2005 when she joined which soap opera?

762. Following on from the previous question, what was the name of Louisa's character, who was the daughter of gangster Johnny?

763. Louisa was born in Camden in which year – 1987, 1988 or 1989?

764. In 2006 Louisa was a contestant on Strictly Come Dancing, but who was her professional dancing partner – Vincent Simone, James Jordan or Erin Boag?

765. In Harry Potter and the Chambers of Secrets Louisa was the double for which French-born British actress who played Hermione Granger?

766. Louisa came 9th out of 14 contestants in which of the following competitions held in Glasgow – Euro Ball Contest, Eurovision Dance Contest or The Euro Dance Along?

767. What is Louisa's middle name – Claire, Carrie or Charmaine?

768. In The British Soap Awards 2006, which award did Louisa win – Best Actress, Sexiest Female or Best Newcomer?

769. True or false: Louisa is of Russian descent on her mother's side?

770. What are the rank and name of Louisa's character in The Bill?

Jack Meadows

771. Jack Meadows is a character in which police drama?

772. In which year did Jack Meadows arrive permanently in Sun Hill – 1992, 1993 or 1994?

773. Meadows had been demoted from which previous position – Detective Constable, Detective Sergeant or Detective Superintendent?

774. What is Meadows' present title – Inspector, Detective Chief Inspector or Chief Inspector?

775. In the 1980s Meadows was part of which squad – Beech Boys, Beagle Boys or Pet Shop Boys?

776. Meadows has a soft spot for which Detective Constable – Don Beech, Mickey Webb or Tom Chandler?

777. Which fast food does Meadows like for lunch?

778. Which football team does Meadows support – Manchester United, Manchester City or Liverpool?

779. Which actor plays Jack Meadows – Clive Wedderburn, Simon Rouse or Mark Rowley?

780. Can you name Jack's ex-wife, to whom he was married for 28 years?

June Ackland

781. In 1983 WPC June Ackland appeared in a pilot episode, called 'Woodentop', of which ITV police drama?

782. Which actress played June Ackland – Trudie Goodwin, Kaye Darling or Lisa Maxwell?

783. June was a WPC from 1983 until 1995, when she was promoted to which position – Sergeant, Detective Constable or Inspector?

784. June's call sign was Sierra Oscar – 38, 48 or 58?

785. Which colleague did June marry and subsequently divorce because of his gambling addiction?

786. Which police constable, played by Todd Carty, tried to convince June that he was her long lost son and in the end committed suicide?

787. June was the last of the original characters after how many years on the show – 21, 22 or 23?

788. Who was to be June's husband upon her retirement – Rod Stewart, Rod Jessop or Rod Steiger?

789. June was the favourite character of which prince – William, Harry or Charles?

790. Which character succeeded June, played by actor Sam Callis?

Terry Perkins

791. Terry Perkins is a character in which ITV police drama?

792. Where was Terry stationed before his transfer to Sun Hill – Barton Street, Burton Street or Breton Street?

793. Terry's first investigation was the rape of which DCI's wife?

794. In which year did Terry arrive, in episode number 165 – 2001, 2003 or 2005?

795. Which actor portrays Terry Perkins – Bruce Byron, Alec Peters or Roger Leach?

796. True or false: Terry married his wife, Helen, for a second time?

797. How many children does Terry have?

798. What are the names of Terry's children?

799. What was the first name of Terry's informant, who died in his arms?

800. What is Terry's title – Detective Constable, Detective Sergeant or Detective Inspector?

Guest Appearances

801. Which pop star appeared in EastEnders' Queen Vic in 1995 – Gary Barlow, Mark Owen or Robbie Williams?

802. Which member of the royal family appeared on Coronation Street in a news report by Trevor McDonald, which celebrated its 40th year?

803. Which Lord of the Rings actor appeared as Mel Hutchwright in Coronation Street?

804. Which actress appeared in Holby City in 2001 as Alex Adam's ex, and later became Connie Beauchamp?

805. Which Titanic actress appeared as Suzanne in Casualty in 1993?

806. Which elf-prince and pirate appeared in Casualty as an extra for three episodes between 1994 and 1996?

807. Which 'badly behaved' man appeared in Neighbours as a priest in 2007 – Neil Morrissey, Martin Clunes or Harry Enfield?

808. Which Australian cricketer appeared twice in Neighbours in 2006 – Shane Warne, Richie Benaud or Dennis Lillee?

809. Which English 'proud but prejudiced' actress played a ten-year-old tearaway called Sheena Rose in The Bill in 1995?

810. Which ex-French, Arsenal and Chelsea midfield footballer appeared in the 1998 Christmas episode of The Bill – Emmanuel Petit, Eric Cantona or Thierry Henry?

Pot Luck – 1

811. In EastEnders, which character celebrated his 40th birthday on Friday 27 February 2009?

812. In Coronation Street, who walked in on Joe and Len shaking hands in Joe's lock-up?

813. In Emmerdale, which two boys fought over Victoria?

814. In Hollyoaks, who lashed out at Lydia when she saw her in a clinch with Josh?

815. In Neighbours, which family left Ramsay Street in 2009 after only two years in the soap?

816. Which ex-Australian Idol contestant joined the cast of Home and Away as rock star Liam Murphy?

817. In Doctors, who treated a patient that claimed to see fairies at the bottom of his garden?

818. Which former Coronation Street actor, who played Vikram Desai, appeared in Casualty on Valentine's Day 2009?

819. Which Holby City actress, who plays Connie, claims to have been snubbed by Dame Judi Dench at the 2008 TV BAFTA awards?

820. Which actress, who played DI Sam Nixon for seven years, departed from The Bill in an explosive storyline?

Pot Luck – 2

821. Who is the father of Bethany Platt from Coronation Street – Neil Ferns, Neil Rose or Neil Woods?

822. What is the name of the fictional tube station in EastEnders?

823. What are the first names of Emmerdale's three King brothers?

824. What is the phone number of Sun Hill Police Station – 020 7511 1642, 020 8622 2753 or 999?

825. In which soap opera does the character Rosie Webster appear?

826. Who is the longest-running UK soap opera actor?

827. What was the name of Gail's mother-in-law, played by Lynne Perrie, in Coronation Street?

828. Which actor played Emmerdale's Joe Sugden – Tony Pitts, Frazer Hines or Niven Boyd?

829. True or false: Johnny Briggs, who played Mike Baldwin in Coronation Street, was a patient in Holby City?

830. Dot Cotton and Lou Beale were Walford's original pensioners in EastEnders, but who was the third one, portrayed by Gretchen Franklin?

Pot Luck – 3

831. Which EastEnders character started 2008 with a metal pole impaled through his stomach?

832. Who came back to EastEnders' Albert Square to announce his father's death in April 2008?

833. Following on from the previous question, which loud-mouthed redhead returned at the same time?

834. As of 2009, who are the current residents of Emmerdale's Home Farm?

835. In Coronation Street, with whom is Ken Barlow having a bit of romantic 'argy-bargy' behind Dierdre's back?

836. Which actor plays Lou Carpenter in Neighbours – Alan Fletcher, Tom Oliver or Ryan Moloney?

837. In Holby City the ambulance vehicles and uniforms derive from which service – Great Western, Great Eastern or Greater London?

838. Home and Away is also the title of an album by which American rocker – Bruce Springsteen, Del Shannon or Lynyrd Skynyrd?

839. Until 2008, which actress played the role of Dr Maggie Coldwell in Casualty – Catherine Cookson, Mary Cookson or Susan Cookson?

840. What was the first name of Ken Barlow's mother in Coronation Street – Edna, Ida or Nancy?

Pot Luck – 4

841. Willy was the name of a famous dog from which soap opera?

842. True or false: Steve Halliwell, who plays Zak Dingle in Emmerdale, is Spice Girl Geri Halliwell's father?

843. In Home and Away, which actress plays Colleen Smart, née Hickie – Lyn Collingwood, Rebecca Breeds or Jodi Gordon?

844. In Coronation Street, who tried to kill Dev and Sunita?

845. True or false: Julie Goodyear, who played Bet Lynch in Coronation Street, was married to Ray Sutcliffe, later to become The Yorkshire Ripper, from 1960 to 1963?

846. In EastEnders, what was the 'devilish' name of Roxy's boyfriend from Ibiza?

847. In Neighbours, which actress portrays Elle Robinson, daughter of Paul Robinson – Jackie Woodburne, Pipa Black or Kym Valentine?

848. In EastEnders, who was buried alive in Epping Forest?

849. In Coronation Street, what is the first name of Deirdre's mother?

850. True or false: the term 'soap opera' originates from radio serials that were sponsored by soap manufacturers such as Proctor and Gamble, Colgate – Palmolive and Lever Brothers?

Love Interests

851. In EastEnders, which 'mechanical' character finally bagged the love of Dawn Swann after coming back from the dead?

852. In Coronation Street, who was the latest disappointment in Gail's Platt's life after the truth came out about his deal with the enemy and his daughter's abortion?

853. In Emmerdale, what is the name of the vet who chased Chas Dingle?

854. In Holby City, which consultant could not convince Faye of his love and bedded Jac?

855. Following on from the previous question, was it Faye or Jac who had an affair with his Lordship's father?

856. Consultant Nick Jordan from Casualty had a love interest with which cardio-thoracic registrar from Holby City?

857. In Coronation Street, whom did Becky kick into touch for Steve McDonald?

858. Following on from the previous question, whom did Steve McDonald dump for Becky?

859. In Emmerdale, which two characters entered into a civil partnership on 3 March 2008, split and almost got divorced, and then flew off to Australia together?

860. In Emmerdale, what is the name of Rodney Blackstock's gold-digging daughter, for whom love always has a price?

Guess The Year

861. In Coronation Street, in which year was Hilda Ogden's last appearance after 23 years – 1987, 1988 or 1989?

862. In EastEnders the rape of Kathy Beale by James Wilmott-Brown was one of the more controversial storylines, but in which year did it occur – 1986, 1988 or 1990?

863. The village of Emmerdale was known as Beckindale until which year – 1984, 1994 or 2004?

864. In which year was Hollyoaks the only soap opera to be nominated in every category at The British Soap Awards, going on to win three at the ceremony – 2005, 2006 or 2007?

865. In Neighbours, in which year did Scott and Charlene get married – 1987, 1989 or 1991?

866. In which year did the actor Simon Baker, currently in the CBS TV series The Mentalist, guest appear as James Healy in Home and Away – 1992, 1994 or 1996?

867. In which year did Dr Brendan 'Mac' McGuire leave Doctors – 2006, 2007 or 2008?

868. In which year did Robson Green become the porter, Jimmy Powell, in Casualty – 1989, 1990 or 1991?

869. In which year did Robert Powell portray Jesus of Nazareth – 1967, 1977 or 1987?

870. In which year did The Bill celebrate its 10th anniversary – 1992, 1993 or 1994?

Locations

871. Albert Square's design is based on which real-life square in Dalston – Fawset, Fassett or Falset?

872. At least two Albert Squares exist in the East End of London. Can you name where one of them is situated?

873. Name the farm where Andy Sugden lives and works in Emmerdale?

874. Following on from the previous question, can you name the estate where the farm is located?

875. In Coronation Street the medical centre/surgery on Rosamund Street used to be a night club called what?

876. Coronation Street was based on which street in Ordsall in an area of Salford – Archie Street, Baker Street or Quay Street?

877. Can you name the real street that is used to represent the fictional Ramsay Street in Neighbours – Pin Oak Court, Pin Ash Court or Pin Pine Court?

878. No. 6 Ranley Mews in Hollyoaks was the former home of which family – Baker, Barnes or Banes?

879. Which soap opera hospital is based on the Bristol Royal Infirmary?

880. Who lives at No. 3 Coronation Street?

Who's Who – 1

881. In Coronation Street, what relation is Tyrone to Jack Duckworth – son, grandson or adopted son?

882. In EastEnders, what relation is Billy Mitchell to Phil Mitchell – brother, nephew or distant cousin?

883. In Emmerdale, what relation is Diane Sugden to Val Pollard?

884. Barry 'Newt' Newton arrived in Hollyoaks in 2007 as what relation to Jack and Frankie Osbourne – long lost son of Frankie, foster child or godson?

885. Actress Anne Charleston arrived in Emmerdale in 2006, but what was the name of the on-screen hus band she left in Neighbours?

886. In Home and Away, what relation is Martha McKenzie to Alf Stewart?

887. In EastEnders, what relation was Pauline Fowler to Ian Beale?

888. In Casualty, Louis is the son of which character – Charlie Fairhead, Ruth Winters or Nick Jordan?

889. In Holby City, Chrissie Williams is portrayed as Mark Williams' daughter, but who is her biological father?

890. In The Bill, what is the name of the daughter of single mother, Samantha Nixon?

Who's Who – 2

891. In Coronation Street, Emily Bishop was known by which name between 1961 and 1969 – Miss Naylor, Miss Nugent or Miss Napier?

892. In EastEnders, what are the names of Ian Beale's parents?

893. Following on from the previous question, can you name Ian Beale's three children?

894. In Emmerdale, Terry Woods had a son called TJ with his former wife Dawn. Who is Dawn's father?

895. Following on from the previous question, can you name her father's twins?

896. Harry Harper left Casualty in 2008, but can you name his daughter?

897. In The Bill, Superintendent Tom Chandler committed suicide in 2002. Can you name the widow he left behind?

898. In Coronation Street, what relation is Bethany to Gail Platt?

899. Following on from the previous question, who is Bethany's mother?

900. True or false: in Emmerdale, one of Annie Brearly's former names was Kempinski?

Deaths

901. Which character in Coronation Street died of a heart attack in the snug of the Rovers Return Inn in 1964 – Ena Sharples, Minnie Caldwell or Martha Longhurst?

902. Name the character in EastEnders who died in 1996 as a result of a blow to the head in a prison riot that led to a brain haemorrhage after his release while he was working on his allotment.

903. Name the Dingle who died in Emmerdale's famous storm of 2003.

904. Which character died twice in EastEnders?

905. In Emmerdale, name the 'superbitch' who watched Frank Tate die of a heart attack?

906. Name the actress from Holby City who died after falling from the balcony of her boyfriend's flat in 2003.

907. In Coronation Street, who was murdered during Tony Gordon's stag night?

908. In 1998, who was killed in Emmerdale by Billy Hopwood during an armed robbery on Christmas Day?

909. In Coronation Street, who died of a massive heart attack in the hallway of Audrey's house in 2006?

910. On Christmas Day 2006, 10.7 million viewers tuned in to witness the death of which character after 22 years in EastEnders?

Early Days

911. In the 1960s, Ena Sharples was the caretaker of which mission hall along with her friends, Minnie and Martha – Happy Tidings, Joyful Tidings or Glad Tidings?

912. Lou Beale was the first EastEnders character to be created, but which actress portrayed her?

913. Continuing from the previous question, the character was also played by which actress in an EastEnders special – Karen Meagher, Karen Meacher or Karen Meaton?

914. Joe Sugden was in Emmerdale between 1972 and 1994. In 1994, where did he move to and how did he die?

915. How many years did Amos Brearly and Henry Wilks run The Woolpack in Emmerdale – 19, 20 or 21 years?

916. The first episode of Emmerdale Farm opened with the funeral of which Sugden character in 1972?

917. Charlie Fairhead married which Casualty character, who left and returned a decade later?

918. Anton Mayer was one of the original cast of Holby City, resulting in the 1999 to 2001 period being known by fans as what 'era'?

919. Name the stand-up comedian and presenter who guest appeared on The Bill in 1984 who resigned from BBC radio 2 after a prank call conducted with Jonathan Ross?

920. Bill Maynard played Coronation Street's Micky Malone in 1970, but what was the name of his character in Heartbeat between 1992 and 2001?

Spin-Offs

921. What is the title of the first spin-off book of Home and Away in 1989 – Home and Away: Behind The Scenes, The Frank Morgan Story or The Bobby Simpson Story?

922. Which 1965-66 sitcom spin-off of Coronation Street starred Arthur Lowe as Leonard Swindley, who was formerly the shopkeeper on Coronation Street – Pardon the Expression, Excuse the Display or Spare the Look?

923. Which revolutionary Irish soap opera, set in Meath, inspired the creation of Emmerdale – The Gordians, The Dorians or The Riordans?

924. Which ill-fated Hollyoaks spin-off featured Ruth Osborne, played by Terri Dwyer, who started a new life in London away from her relationship with Lewis Richardson – Hollyoaks: Moving On, Hollyoaks: Let Loose or Hollyoaks: In the City?

925. Name the 1999 Casualty spin-off, which has occasional crossover mini-dramas with Casualty.

926. Name the EastEnders show available to digital viewers and presented by Angellica Bell?

927. What are the titles of the historical medical dramas, which are an extension of Casualty, set in The Royal London Hospital 100 years previously?

928. Which spin-off show from The Bill in 2003 investigated the drive-by shooting of Sgt Matthew Boyden – Burnside, Beech is Back or MIT: Murder Investigation Team?

929. What was the title of the charity crossover between EastEnders and Doctor Who in November 1993 in aid of Children in Need – Dimensions in Time, Measurements in Time or Magnitude in Time?

930. Which EastEnders' special was based on a character's childhood experiences of evacuation to Wales during World War II – Dot's Story, Peggy's Story or Ethel's Story?

Reveal The Character – 1

931. Rearrange the following letters to reveal an EastEnders catering magnet – NAI ELAEB.

932. Rearrange the following letters to reveal Coronation Street's queen of the hotpot – BYETT ASWILLIM.

933. Rearrange the following letters to reveal the cheating swindler of Emmerdale – REIC DOLLARP.

934. Rearrange the following letters to reveal a teacher from Hollyoaks – USSR NOEW.

935. Rearrange the following letters to reveal the newsman of Erinsborough – ALUP BORINNOS.

936. Rearrange the following letters to reveal a resident of Summer Bay House in Home and Away – LAF TWARTES.

937. Rearrange the following letters to reveal a Doctors character played by Diane Keen – ALUJI ONSPARS.

938. Rearrange the following letters to reveal a paramedic from Casualty – EFJF LOCLIRE.

939. Rearrange the following letters to reveal a 'she devil' registrar who bedded a father and son – CAJ LOYNAR.

940. Rearrange the following letters to reveal this female adopted detective constable, played by Cat Simmons, who joined The Bill in 2006 – AZEKI KERWAL.

Reveal The Character – 2

941. Rearrange the following letters to reveal the first landlady of the Rovers Return in Coronation Street – NIENA KALREW.

942. Rearrange the following letters to reveal a cabbie from Albert Square – ARCHIEL LATERS.

943. Rearrange the following letters to reveal a former co-landlord of The Woolpack in Emmerdale – MOSA LYE BARR.

944. Rearrange the following letters to reveal a member of 'The Dirty Diegos' in Hollyoaks – SYRH SHOWRATH.

945. Rearrange the following letters to reveal the young character who lives at No. 28 Ramsay Street with Susan and Karl – KEZE NIKSIK.

946. Rearrange the following letters to reveal the character played by Josh Quong Tart in Home and Away – SEMIL DELOPANC.

947. Rearrange the following letters to reveal a 'jack the lad' practice nurse at the Doctors Mill Health Centre – IREACH MALHAL.

948. Rearrange the following letters to reveal a female medicine-stealing paramedic from Casualty – ANENZAS OVALLIC.

949. Rearrange the following letters to reveal a Filipino ward sister from Holby's Keller Ward – SHADIA DANSENOR.

950. Rearrange the following letters to reveal a former police sergeant in The Bill who was promoted to inspector to replace Gina Gold – CHELAR NOSTEW.

Match The Character – 1

Match up the character with the correct soap opera

951. Mo Harris

952. Roy Cropper

953. Daz Eden

954. Hugo Austin

955. Karen Hollins

956. Sally Armstrong

957. Alice Chantrey

958. Paul Rose

959. Leo Valentine

960. Sam Clark

Soaps: Doctors, Emmerdale, Hollyoaks, Neighbours, The Bill, Casualty, EastEnders, Coronation Street, Holby City, Home and Away

Match The Character – 2

Match up the character with the correct soap opera

961. Betty Williams

962. Linda Clarke

963. Shane Doyle

964. Tony Hutchinson

965. Steve Parker

966. Irene Roberts

967. Ronnie Woodson

968. Jessica Harrison

969. Maria Kendall

970. Eddie Olosunje

Soaps: Home and Away, Doctors, The Bill, Casualty, Holby City, Coronation Street, EastEnders, Hollyoaks, Neighbours, Emmerdale

The Queen Victoria

971. Name the carpenter, played by Oscar James, hired by Den Watts to remove the pub's interior partition in 1985?

972. The Queen Victoria is often referred to in which two abbreviated forms?

973. True or false: in 1998, Bianca Butcher gave birth to baby Liam on Christmas day inside the Queen Vic?

974. What was the original name of The Queen Victoria?

975. In the 1980s, what colour was The Queen Victoria painted?

976. Who set fire to The Queen Victoria for insurance money?

977. Who were the first landlords of The Queen Victoria?

978. Eddie Royle became the landlord in 1990 but was murdered by which character after just one year in charge?

979. Can you name the pot man who died of a heart attack in the gentleman's toilet in 1988?

980. As of March 2009, who is the licensee of The Queen Victoria?

Rovers Return Inn

981. In which year was the Rovers Return Inn built and run by Jim Corbishley for 17 years – 1900, 1902 or 1904?

982. The Rovers Return Inn occupies the corner of which two streets?

983. The Rovers Return Inn was originally owned by which fictional brewery?

984. In which year did the Rovers Return Inn become a free house – 1992, 1994 or 1996?

985. Annie Walker was the landlady for how many years – 26, 36 or 46?

986. Who was arguably the most famous barmaid of the Rovers Return Inn?

987. Which popular culinary delight is a mainstay of the Rovers Return Inn fare – pie and mash, cottage pie or hotpot?

988. Mike Baldwin and Duggie Ferguson bought the Rovers Return Inn in 2001, but who was the third person in the three-man consortium?

989. True or false: the Rovers Return Inn was originally to be called The Coronation?

990. In 2006 Liz McDonald became the landlady of the Rovers Return Inn, but who actually bought it?

The Woolpack

991. The first Woolpack was which inn based in Arncliffe – the Parrot Inn, the Falcon Inn or the osprey Inn?

992. What was the name of the second pub that was used for The Woolpack?

993. Which village first played host to The Woolpack – Esholt, Evesholt or Evensholt?

994. What was the name of The Woolpack's rival public house, which was supposedly downmarket?

995. As a result of the 1993 plane crash, which character became paralysed from the waist down after being trapped inside The Woolpack's wine bar?

996. In 1973, which duo became the landlords of The Woolpack?

997. True or false: following on from the previous question, the duo were held at gun point in a robbery in 1978?

998. Which gamekeeper appeared in 1980 to become one of the most well-known locals – Frank Tate, Seth Armstrong or Eric Pollard?

999. In 1999, which two Blackstocks became landladies?

1000. On which estate is The Woolpack now situated – Halewood, Harwood or Harewood?

Answers

Eastenders

1. 1985 (19 February)

2. Tony Holland and Julia Smith

3. The Queen Victoria public house

4. Civvy Street

5. Victoria Road and Turpin Road

6. Dennis Watts

7. Bench of Tears

8. On Christmas Day

9. Emma Bunton

10. Lisa Shaw (his former girlfriend)

Coronation Street

11. 1960

12. Tony Warren

13. Granada Television

14. Weatherfield

15. Jubilee Street

16. Rosamund Street, Victoria Street and Viaduct Street

17. True

18. The Kabin

19. Vera Duckworth

20. Eric Spear

Emmerdale

Hollyoaks

31. United Kingdom

32. 1995

33. Cheshire

34. Tony Hutchinson

35. 4

36. True

37. Niall Rafferty

38. Hollyoaks: Later

39. 6

40. Hollyoaks Community College

Neighbours

Home And Away

51. 1988

52. Sydney

53. Pippa and Tom Fletcher

54. The Stewart family

55. Alan Bateman

56. True

57. 7

58. Dannii

59. Alf Stewart

60. Jack Holden

Doctors

61. 2000

62. The Mill

63. False

64. 6 years

65. George, Ronnie and Nick

66. Ireland

67. Todd Carty

68. Sergeant Vic Scott

69. Ronnie Woodson

70. Leo

Casualty

71. 1986

72. True

73. Holby City

74. Accident and Emergency

75. Jeremy Brock and Paul Unwin

76. True

77. Holby Blue

78. Charlie Fairhead

79. 5

80. Ken Freeman

Holby City

81. 1999

82. Tony Hale and Mal Young

83. Wyvern

84. Keller, Darwin and Otter

85. Chrissie Williams

86. BAFTA TV Award

87. True

88. Michael French and Paul Bradley

89. Mark Williams

90. Fuel tanker

The Bill

91. 1994

92. True

93. Geoff McQueen

94. Sun Hill

95. Canley

96. Kevin Lloyd

97. True

98. Emma Bunton

99. EastEnders (as Ruby Allen)

100. 3

Leslie Grantham

101. 1947

102. False: he was born in Camberwell

103. Royal Fusiliers

104. True

105. Dr Who

106. 20

107. The Bill

108. Danny Kane

109. Life and Other Times

110. True

Mike Reid

111. EastEnders

112. Frank Butcher

113. 1940

114. True

115. 'The Ugly Duckling'

116. 1987

117. 2000

118. True

119. Golf

120. Spain

Wendy Richard

Pam St Clement

131. Pat Evans

132. 1986

133. Frank

134. True

135. Teacher

136. Emmerdale

137. Islington

138. 1942

139. False: Adam Woodyatt is the longest-serving cast member

140. Wicks

'Dirty Den'

141. 1985

142. Dennis Watts

143. True

144. Roly

145. Anita Dobson

146. Michelle Fowler

147. Jan Hammond

148. Daffodils

149. Spain

150. Chrissie (his second wife)

Dawn Swann

151. EastEnders

152. Kara Tointon

153. 2005

154. True

155. Rob Minter

156. Dr May Wright

157. Garry Hobbs and Jase Dyer

158. Jase Dyer

159. Jay (Jase Dyer's son)

160. Argee Bargee

Phil Mitchell

161. Steve McFadden

162. 1990

163. Grant

164. 3

165. Sharon

166. Turpin Way

167. Ben

168. Nadia Borovac, from Romania

169. Lorna Cartwright

170. True

William Roache

171. Coronation Street

172. 1960

173. True

174. 1932

175. Patrick

176. True

177. Lifetime Achievement

178. Conservative

179. No. 1

180. Teacher

John Savident

181. Coronation Street

182. 1938

183. Guernsey

184. Policeman

185. A Clockwork Orange

186. 1968

187. Butcher

188. True

189. 2005

190. Heart attack

Elizabeth (Liz) Dawn

191. 1939

192. Silvia Butterfield

193. Leeds

194. Coronation Street

195. Vera Duckworth

196. True

197. Leeds

198. MBE

199. 2008

200. Jack Duckworth

Julie Goodyear

201. Lancashire

202. 1940s (1942)

203. Kemp

204. MBE

205. Just Julie

206. True

207. Hollyoaks

208. Marlene Dietrich

209. Shredded Wheat

210. 1 stone 10 pounds

Elsie Tanner

211. Coronation Street

212. Patricia Phoenix

213. True

214. 1984

215. Portugal

216. True

217. Arnold Tanner

218. Miami Modes

219. Len Fairclough

220. False: it was pear and ginger

Mike Baldwin

221. Johnny Briggs

222. 1976

223. Ken Barlow

224. 3

225. Deirdre and Susan (Ken's daughter) and Susan had a son (Adam) by him

226. Underworld

227. Alma

228. Heart attack

229. (A)

230. 2006

Bet Lynch

231. Coronation Street

232. Julie Goodyear

233. 1966

234. Annie Walker

235. True

236. Alec Gilroy

237. 1992

238. Jack and Vera Duckworth

239. Jim McDonald

240. Leopard

Patrick Mower

Ronald Magill

251. Emmerdale Farm

252. Hull

253. True

254. Royal Signals

255. 1972

256. Henry Wilks

257. Julius Caesar

258. His long, bushy sideburns

259. Wogan

260. Annie

Elizabeth Estensen

261. Emmerdale

262. 1949

263. Geordie

264. The Liver Birds

265. Polly James

266. T-Bag

267. Coronation Street

268. Billy Hopwood

269. True

270. 1999

Lucy Pargeter

Jack Sugden

281. Andrew Burt

282. Farmer

283. London

284. Italy

285. Clive Hornby

286. Tares in the Field

287. 3

288. Robert and Victoria

289. Andy

290. Spain

Jasmine Thomas

291. Emmerdale

292. Jenna-Louise Coleman

293. 2005

294. Revd Ashley Thomas

295. Hotton Courier

296. Tom King

297. Nicola Blackstock

298. Shane Doyle (policeman)

299. Debbie and Eli Dingle

300. Scotland

Zak Dingle

301. Emmerdale

302. 1994

303. 1952

304. Wishing Well Cottage

305. Lisa

306. Steve Halliwell

307. Chile

308. Bare knuckle

309. Ben and Butch

310. True

Chris Fountain

John Pickard

321. Dominic Reilly

322. 2005

323. Chef

324. Tony Hutchinson

325. True

326. 10

327. EastEnders

328. Neil Timpson

329. True

330. Tottenham Hotspur

Sarah Jayne Dunn

331. Hollyoaks

332. Mandy Richardson

333. 1996

334. 2006

335. Doctors

336. 1981

337. Becca Dean

338. The Dark Knight

339. Vauxhall Crossed

340. False

Samantha Giles

Tony Hutchinson

351. False: Hollyoaks

352. Nick Pickard

353. 1995

354. Chef

355. Mandy Richardson

356. Harry

357. Jasmine Bates

358. Gordon Cunningham

359. Grace Antonia Helen

360. Dom

Steph Cunningham

361. Hollyoaks

362. Carley Stenson

363. 2000

364. Stephanie De La Dean

365. True

366. Epilepsy

367. A donkey

368. Wedding day

369. Struck by a car

370. Brother

Darren Osbourne

371. Hollyoaks

372. Adam Booth

373. Ashley Taylor Dawson

374. The Dog in the Pond

375. 4

376. Sam Owen

377. Gambling

378. True

379. 20

380. Toilet cleaner

Jason Donavan

381. Scott Robinson

382. Sean

383. 1968

384. True: Terence Donavan (who played Doug Willis in Neighbours)

385. Kylie Minogue

386. 'Especially for You'

387. True

388. Joseph, in Joseph and the Amazing Technicolor Dreamcoat

389. I'm a Celebrity ... Get Me Out of Here

390. Echo Beach

Alan Dale

391. Jim

392. New Zealand

393. Rugby

394. The Young Doctors

395. America

396. True

397. Vice President Jim Prescott

398. Kiss 100

399. Gene Hackman

400. Heart attack

Kylie Minogue

401. Charlene Mitchell

402. 1986

403. OBE

404. Stock, Aitken and Waterman

405. 'I Should Be So Lucky'

406. 'Loco-Motion'

407. Showgirl

408. True: her mother was born in Wales

409. Florence

410. La La La

Holly Valance

411. Neighbours

412. 1983

413. Vukadinovic

414. False: Benny Hill's cousin

415. Music

416. Model

417. 'Kiss Kiss'

418. Footprints

419. 2004

420. Taken

Paul Robinson

421. Neighbours

422. Stefan Dennis

423. 1985

424. True

425. J.R. Ewing

426. An airline steward

427. Hawaii

428. 2004

429. Harold Bishop

430. 2

Madge Bishop

431. Neighbours

432. Anne Charleston

433. 1986

434. 11

435. 24

436. Max Ramsay

437. Kylie Minogue (Charlene)

438. Harold Bishop

439. Fred Mitchell

440. Terminal cancer

Karl Kennedy

441. Neighbours

442. Alan Fletcher

443. 1994

444. Doctor

445. False: Raymond

446. Karl Marx

447. London

448. Emma Bunton

449. The Right Prescription

450. True

Dannii Minogue

451. Emma Jackson

452. Love and Kisses

453. The Sullivans

454. Younger

455. The X Factor

456. True

457. True

458. Jacques Villeneuve

459. Top of the Pops

460. True

Heath Ledger

461. Scott Irwin

462. 1997

463. Chess

464. Andrew

465. Perth

466. 1979

467. 19

468. Brokeback Mountain

469. The Dark Knight

470. 28

Lynne Mcgranger

471. Home and Away

472. 1953

473. Wagga Wagga

474. The Flying Doctors

475. 1993

476. The Morning Show

477. Partner of the pier diner

478. Jacqui Phillips

479. Robert De Niro

480. Blonde

Naomi Watts

481. Home and Away

482. Julie Gibson, 1991

483. True

484. Pink Floyd

485. False: England (Shoreham, Kent)

486. Tank Girl

487. Ann Darrow

488. Fame

489. Japan

490. Liev Schreiber

Colleen Smart

491. Home and Away

492. Lyn Collingwood

493. 1999

494. Waitress

495. Morag Stewart

496. Johnny Cooper

497. Sticky Beak

498. Miss Groper

499. True

500. True

Alfred 'Alf' Stewart

501. Entrepreneur

502. Ray Meagher

503. 1988

504. Douglas

505. Martha and Ailsa

506. Drowned

507. 2000

508. Stewie

509. Bridget Simmons

510. Owen

Aden Jefferies

511. Home and Away

512. Todd Lasance

513. Worker on a prawn fishing boat

514. His grandfather

515. Sean and Justin

516. The Harris family

517. 2005

518. Susan 'Belle' Taylor

519. Nicole Franklin

520. Joey

Christopher Timothy

521. Doctors

522. Dr Brendan 'Mac' McGuire

523. 1940

524. Welsh

525. All Creatures Great and Small

526. Vet

527. Finlay Newton

528. True: Andrew Timothy

529. Chris Collins

530. Z Cars

Matt Kennard

531. Doctors

532. 2007

533. Jimmy Mullins

534. The Bill

535. Duncan Edwards

536. Sam

537. Heartbeat

538. 1982

539. Grimsby

540. Nurse

Angela Lonsdale

541. Policewoman

542. DI Eva Moore

543. 2007

544. False: she was born in the Lake District (Penrith) but did not appear in the series

545. Emma Watts

546. Curly Watts

547. Billy (Perry Fenwick)

548. A Touch of Frost

549. Sunderland

550. False: she played Helen, the ex-wife of DC Terry Perkins

Emma Samms

551. Doctors

552. Jimmy Clay

553. 1960

554. Samuelson

555. Hip

556. General Hospital

557. Dynasty

558. The Colbys

559. Holby City

560. The Bill

Adrian Lewis Morgan

561. Dr Jimmi Clay

562. Police surgeon

563. 1973

564. False: Welsh

565. Holby City

566. Liam Evans

567. Roger

568. 12 Angry Men

569. Les Misérables

570. 2005

Diane Keen

571. Doctors

572. 1946

573. The Sex Thief

574. Emmerdale Farm

575. Nescafé

576. Brookside

577. The Sandbaggers

578. Inspector Wexford

579. True

580. Paul Greenwood

Anita Carey

581. Vivian March

582. Receptionist

583. True

584. Casualty

585. Coronation Street

586. Dixon of Dock Green

587. Still Crazy

588. Final Fantasy 12

589. False

590. Bob Dylan

Simon Maccorkindale

591. Casualty

592. 2002

593. 2008

594. Eyesight test

595. Falcon Crest

596. 1952

597. Fiona Fullerton

598. Susan George

599. Fiji

600. Jesus of Nazareth

Charles Dale

601. Casualty

602. Big Mac (Mackenzie 'Big Mac' Chalker)

603. Welsh

604. The Lakes

605. Coronation Street

606. The Eustace Brothers

607. 3

608. Rocket Man

609. True

610. 1963

Caroline Langrishe

Leanne Wilson

621. Casualty

622. Doctors

623. Tracker

624. True

625. 70th

626. The Holiday

627. Stars in Fast Cars

628. Dennis Waterman

629. Dog

630. Builder

Charlie Fairhead

631. Casualty

632. Derek Thompson

633. 1986

634. Senior charge nurse

635. Barbara 'Baz' Wilder

636. Louis

637. Reliant Scimitar

638. Morris Traveller

639. True

640. Casualty@HolbyCity

Ruth Winters

641. Casualty

642. Junior doctor

643. 2007

644. Georgia Taylor

645. 8

646. Toby De Silva

647. Her estranged father

648. Her misdiagnosis of a patient

649. Toby and Abs

650. Toyah Battersby

Josh Griffiths

651. Casualty

652. Ian Bleasdale

653. Paramedic

654. Helen

655. Sarah and Ashley

656. House fire

657. False: he received it from the Queen

658. Laura

659. Pakistan

660. Devika

Paul Bradley

661. EastEnders

662. Elliot Hope

663. Gina

664. True

665. The Kippers

666. The Pianist

667. Ireland

668. Red Dwarf

669. True

670. 1955

Robert Powell

Patsy Kensit

681. Emmerdale

682. Holby City

683. Casualty

684. Eighth Wonder

685. 'I'm Not Scared'

686. Love and Betrayal

687. Jimmy The Dip

688. False: he was named Lennon after John Lennon

689. Liam Gallagher

690. Reggie

Sharon D. Clarke

691. Holby City

692. 2005

693. Keller Ward

694. Last Choir Standing

695. Boo!

696. The Lion King

697. Matron Mama Morton

698. We Will Rock You

699. Nomad

700. 'Mad World'

'Abra' Durant

701. Holby City

702. Percival

703. Adrian 'Ade' Edmondson

704. 2005

705. 6

706. Kyla Tyson

707. Diane Lloyd

708. Pig

709. Kyle

710. Troublemaker

Rick Griffin

711. Holby City

712. Hugh Quarshie

713. Kobina Eric

714. 2001

715. 'Rogue Males'

716. True

717. Ghana

718. False: he runs a hospital

719. 5

720. Paris Khan

Jayne Grayson

721. Holby City

722. 2007

723. 'Under the Radar'

724. Scottish

725. Christopher Sutherland

726. Casualty

727. True

728. Connie Beauchamp

729. Linden Cullen

730. Stella Gonet

Patrick Robinson

731. Martin 'Ash' Ashford

732. Leon Washington

733. Thomas Peters

734. The Bill

735. Banksy

736. False: he is the cousin of Ian Wright

737. 1963

738. Romeo & Juliet

739. Riverdance

740. Barrister

Daniel Flynn

741. Superintendent John Heaton

742. 2006

743. 52

744. Jerome

745. True

746. Serena Evans

747. False

748. Oliver Cromwell

749. Ginger

750. The Bill

Gina Gold

751. The Bill

752. 2002

753. Inspector

754. 3

755. 2008

756. Retirement

757. False

758. Roberta Taylor

759. Smithy

760. EastEnders

Louisa Lytton

761. EastEnders

762. Ruby Allen

763. 1989

764. Vincent Simone

765. Emma Watson

766. Eurovision Dance Contest

767. Claire

768. Sexiest Female

769. False: she is of Italian descent

770. PC Beth Green

Jack Meadows

771. The Bill

772. 1992

773. Detective Superintendent

774. Detective Chief Inspector

775. Beagle Boys

776. Mickey Webb

777. Fish and chips

778. Manchester United

779. Simon Rouse

780. Laura

June Ackland

Terry Perkins

791. The Bill

792. Barton Street

793. Jack Meadows

794. 2003

795. Bruce Byron

796. True

797. 2

798. Holly and Shaun

799. Barry

800. Detective Constable

Guest Appearances

801. Robbie Williams

802. Prince Charles

803. Ian McKellen

804. Amanda Mealing

805. Kate Winslet

806. Orlando Bloom

807. Neil Morrissey

808. Shane Warne

809. Keira Knightley

810. Emmanuel Petit

Pot Luck – 1

811. Ian Beale

812. David

813. Daz and Aaron

814. Amy

815. The Parker family

816. Axle Whitehead

817. Michelle

818. Chris Bisson

819. Amanda Mealing

820. Lisa Maxwell

Pot Luck – 2

821. Neil Ferns

822. Walford East

823. Matthew, Jimmy and Carl

824. 020 7511 1642

825. Coronation Street

826. William Roache (Coronation Street)

827. Ivy Tilsley

828. Frazer Hines

829. True

830. Ethel Skinner

Pot Luck – 3

831. Kevin Wicks

832. Ricky Butcher

833. Bianca Jackson

834. Mark and Natasha Wylde and children Maisie, Will and Nathan

835. Martha Fraser

836. Tom Oliver

837. Great Western

838. Del Shannon

839. Susan Cookson

840. Ida

Pot Luck – 4

841. EastEnders

842. False: her father is Laurence Francis Halliwell

843. Lyn Collingwood

844. Maya Sharma

845. False

846. Damien

847. Pipa Black

848. Max Branning

849. Blanche

850. True

Love Interests

Guess The Year

861. 1987

862. 1988

863. 1994

864. 2007

865. 1987

866. 1994

867. 2006

868. 1989

869. 1977

870. 1994

Locations

Who's Who – 1

881. Adopted son

882. Distant cousin

883. Sister

884. Foster child

885. Harold Bishop

886. Granddaughter

887. Auntie

888. Charlie Fairhead

889. Frank Williams, Mark's father

890. Abi

Who's Who – 2

891. Miss Nugent

892. Pete and Kathy

893. Lucy, Peter and Bobby

894. Bob Hope

895. Cathy and Heathcliffe

896. Natalya or 'Tally'

897. DS Debbie McAllister

898. Granddaughter

899. Sarah

900. True

Deaths

901. Martha Longhurst

902. Arthur Fowler

903. Tricia Dingle

904. Dennis Watts

905. Kim Tate

906. Laura Sadler

907. Liam Connor

908. Vic Windsor

909. Fred Elliot

910. Pauline Fowler

Early Days

911. Glad Tidings

912. Anna Wing

913. Karen Meagher

914. Spain, car crash

915. 19

916. Jacob

917. Barbara 'Baz' Wilder

918. 'Mayer'

919. Russell Brand

920. Claude Jeremiah Greengrass

Spin-Offs

921. Home and Away: Behind The Scenes

922. Pardon the Expression

923. The Riordans

924. Hollyoaks: Moving On

925. Holby City

926. EastEnders Xtra

927. Casualty 1906, Casualty 1907 and Casualty 1908

928. MIT: Murder Investigation Team

929. Dimensions in Time

930. Dot's Story

Reveal The Character – 1

931. Ian Beale

932. Betty Williams

933. Eric Pollard

934. Russ Owen

935. Paul Robinson

936. Alf Stewart

937. Julia Parsons

938. Jeff Collier

939. Jac Naylor

940. Kezia Walker

Reveal The Character – 2

941. Annie Walker

942. Charlie Slater

943. Amos Brearly

944. Rhys Ashworth

945. Zeke Kinski

946. Miles Copeland

947. Archie Hallam

948. Snezana Lalovic

949. Daisha Anderson

950. Rachel Weston

Match The Character – 1

951. Mo Harris EastEnders

952. Roy Cropper Coronation Street

953. Daz Eden Emmerdale

954. Hugo Austin Home and Away

955. Karen Hollins Doctors

956. Sally Armstrong The Bill

957. Alice Chantrey Casualty

958. Paul Rose Holby City

959. Leo Valentine Hollyoaks

960. Sam Clark Neighbours

Match The Character – 2

961. Betty Williams Coronation Street

962. Linda Clarke EastEnders

963. Shane Doyle Emmerdale

964. Tony Hutchinson Hollyoaks

965. Steve Parker Neighbours

966. Irene Roberts Home and Away

967. Ronnie Woodson Doctors

968. Jessica Harrison Casualty

969. Maria Kendall Holby City

970. Eddie Olosunje The Bill

The Queen Victoria

971. Tony Carpenter

972. The Vic or The Queen Vic

973. True

974. The Balmoral

975. Brown

976. Grant Mitchell

977. Den and Angie Watts

978. Nick Cotton

979. Tom Clements

980. Peggy Mitchell

Rovers Return Inn

981. 1902

982. Coronation Street and Rosamund Street

983. Newton and Ridley

984. 1996

985. 46

986. Bet Lynch

987. Hotpot

988. Fred Elliot

989. True

990. Steve McDonald

The Woolpack

991. Falcon Inn

992. Commercial Inn

993. Esholt

994. The Malt Shovel

995. Chris Tate

996. Amos Brearly and Henry Wilks

997. True

998. Seth Armstrong

999. Diane and Bernice

1000. Harewood

You may also enjoy...

THE REALITY TELEVISION

QUIZ BOOK

1,000 QUESTIONS ON REALITY TV SHOWS

COMPILED BY CHRIS COWLIN
FOREWORD BY CHRISTOPHER BIGGINS

Lightning Source UK Ltd.
Milton Keynes UK
UKHW041552141218
334022UK00001B/31/P

9 780993 337178